SEARCHING FOR A
SUPER MAN
WATCHING FOR A
WONDER WOMAN

Prepare To Find
The *Love* You Desire

SEARCHING FOR A
SUPER MAN
WATCHING FOR A
WONDER WOMAN

Prepare To Find
The *Love* You Desire

Kenn Kington

With Daily Devotional & Small Group Guide

ACKNOWLEDGEMENTS

This project would not exists without God's gracious, patient hand guiding a clueless, hopeless guy into the reality of God's most wonderful truth. Thanks to God first and foremost for His individual, intimate, intricate grace and wisdom. This work would also not exist had God not brought the most wonderful woman in the world into my life. Heather is such a champion for living the truth. We worked through this material together when we met, during the dating stages and have been ever since. She is also an honest and gracious editor. Most of all, her input, encouragement and support helped make an overwhelming task a reality. Heather thanks for being my best friend and a beautiful example of what a wonder woman should look like.

A very special thanks is also in order for my project editor Theresa Druckenmiller. Her endless patience and gifted eye made this work so much better than I had even hoped. Her calm acceptance and focus of my many faults and tangents consistently kept this on course. She is a pleasure and joy to work with.

A special thanks to Shawn Schantz is also in order. His creative edit brought so much to the quality of the work you now hold. It was a pain-staking task to translate my talks into written form. Shawn made this process make sense. His talent as a writer is so impressive and refined. I am honored that he would take the time to invest that talent in this project.

Thanks also to the many friends who have given honest input, offered countless prayers, and encouraged me over the three years this project took to complete. I can honestly say super men and wonder women surround me.

PREFACE

I am so impressed you took the time to read this section. To be completely honest, you have just clued into the most important aspect of this book—without having to wait until the end to figure it out! There is one element that is an absolute necessity for this philosophy to work in your life. I am going to spill the beans right here in the often skipped section called the preface. This secret element is simple, yet complex, and is discovered by understanding the class of reading this book is.

This book is NOT to be read and pondered. If intellectual and theological stimulation is your goal, pick up a copy of Plato and look for the hidden meanings. This book is written for one reason...finding the truths that make relationships workable and fulfilling.

The effectiveness of this book is based on one simple premise. YOU have to apply the truth. I wish it was as easy as thinking the right thoughts, talking to the right people, or agreeing with the right truth. It is not. The only way these principles will work is if you actively, passionately, purposefully, consistently (and any other "ly" ending words you can think of) Do It!!!

A note of encouragement. Rest assured that you will fall short, and it will not come to you naturally. (Wow, thanks for the boost of confidence?!). This quest is not for the passive or faint-hearted. This book is for people who desire real answers and solutions that work. The material covered is not a theologically profound work. It is a first hand encounter this writer had with God directing him (me) from a state of "cluelessness" to being happily married in a wonderful, growing relationship.

The magic is not found in the guidance of the words in this book, or in the examples of trials, shortfalls, and successes, yet hopefully they will be encouraging and helpful. The magic is in the encounter you will have with the living, loving God of all if you choose to learn and live these (His) truths. It will be a fun journey, and I look forward to hearing how God works in your life.

Here we go...

TABLE OF CONTENTS

Introduction... 1

Section 1- Defining Love

Chapter 1: What is Love?... 6
    You Write the Definition

Chapter 2: Microwavable Minute Rice................................. 10
    Complete Commitment

Chapter 3: Sharing Tongues... 16
    Getting Real

Chapter 4: I Just Wanted to Be With You............................ 24
    Giving Unconditionally

Section 2- Understanding Love

Chapter 5: Big Macs and Vitamins.................................... 32
    Fundamental vs. Supplemental Needs

Chapter 6: Road Map to Love... 42
    Defining and Becoming the Character of Love

Chapter 7: Time to Join AAA.. 52
    Constructing Relationships

Section 3-Becoming Love

Chapter 8: Becoming a Great Lover.................................... 66
    Equations to Becoming a Great Lover

Chapter 9: Attitude of Gratitude....................................... 78
    Secrets of Love: Expect Nothing and Appreciate Everything

Chapter 10: A Plan and A Promise..................................... 90
    Relationships: Time, Effort, and Reward

Chapter 11: Completely Trusting....................................... 104
    Pursuit Principles

Chapter 12: How About Those Fries?.................................. 112
    Personal Evaluation and Practical Application

Daily Devotional... 119

Core Group Guide.. 157

INTRODUCTION

I was standing on a small board over 100 feet in the air, waiting to jump on to a trapeze. This is not my idea of fun. I am not afraid of heights by nature, I am, however, not crazy about the idea of free falling ten stories only to become one with the earth.

Why was I there? While standing on the ground with a crowd of well-wishers, it had seemed like a great idea. I guess I wanted to be able to say I had experienced the world's highest man-made element. That my sweet, little wife had just mastered this horrifying feat added more than just a little pressure.

That same nervous excitement is how I often faced relationships. I wanted so badly to experience the love and acceptance we fundamentally long for, yet I feared the pain of a relationship "free fall" with a big 'splat.' Splatting, however, was not new to me. I had practice in two areas that taught me volumes.

I held two impressive records with roommates and former girlfriends. See if you can top them. I have had eighteen roommates in my life, including college. Over nine years that may seem like a lot, and… it is. It is not that I am a hard person to live with; it's that I married off sixteen of these guys. I should have bought stock in a tuxedo company for all the weddings I have been in.

The other record is even worse. Out of the seven women I dated seriously, six of them not only dropped me, but married the next guy they dated. This was devastating, and I have no explanation for this phenomenon. I often pondered these statistics and wondered what was it about me that caused this. These indicators, along with other faults, pointed to the obvious: I was a long way from where I needed to be.

This situation may or may not sound familiar, but parts of it happen to everyone desiring a relationship. How is it that a person can come into an office or classroom one week saying, "Oh, I am in love. He (or she) is so wonderful,"? They continue on and on floating through each day dreaming of the times they will once again be with their "dream come true." Two weeks later, the perfect love hits a big reality speed bump and the relationship comes to a screeching halt. The former dreamer spins emotionally out of control and wishes his or her former dream date would die a slow, painful death.

The vast majority of people have a genuine desire to be in a loving, growing, relationship. So why is love so difficult?

I began to honestly ask this question, and I sought a clear answer. What I found was that relationships were neither meant to be a perpetual frustration in life, nor are they the ultimate answer to complete happiness. Fulfillment and love are not contingent upon the uncontrollable actions and reactions of others.

I cannot tell you the number of times I've heard the questions, "Where are all the great men?" or "Where have all the good women gone?" There is a pervading attitude that our "relationship happiness" is determined by something we have no control over.

This attitude held me captive for a long time. I began to ask God to show me what I could do and what I needed to change. The revolutionary discoveries are in the pages ahead. These truths can radically change your life as well, but only if you allow them to.

If you choose to act on the biblically-based truths shared in this book, God will focus your mind to a complete understanding of how He desires we pursue relationships. He will direct your heart to understand the character required. And, He will guide you clearly to the actions needed to get you to the place you need to be relationally. Let God focus your mind, direct your heart, and guide your steps to the most fulfilling relationships possible.

DEFIING LOVE

CHAPTER ONE

What Is Love?

You Write The Definition

I love chocolate-chip cookie dough ice cream. I love my wife. I love hitting a good drive on a par five. I love my four and a half pound Yorky named Polo. I love large ground beef pizzas. I love my mom and dad. What exactly is love? There are certainly different types, but what about the love deep inside I really desire? So often we say we want to find love, but where is it hiding? We invest great amounts of time, money, and energy seeking love. We risk hurt and embarrassment trying to grasp love. Yet, if we are honest, we may have a difficult time defining what love is exactly.

If we are ever going to find genuine love, we must first learn, then embrace a biblically-based definition of love.

Before we dive right into the definition derived from months of study and application, let's work together for a moment and set our minds in that direction. This may be the only book you ever read where the first chapter is only two pages long, and you actually write part of the chapter. Rest easy that I will write all of the next eleven chapters, but here is your opportunity and assignment. Define love. In your own words, what are the qualities that define love?

Love is:

What are some of the influences on your definition of love?

Now write how you think God would define love.

Are there any basic truths or biblical references you can note to support how you think God would define love? (List them here)

(Do not go on until you have written your part of this chapter.)

Now you can relax and enjoy the rest of the book.

Was it easy coming up with a definition of love? Does your definition and God's sound alike? If this exercise is not easy for you, take heart. Most people have a hard time putting into words what love actually is. How can we find something when we are not really sure what it is? This is the starting point God brought me to after becoming open and honest with Him about my desire to learn and change.

The next few chapters will give the definition He laid upon my heart through numerous verses over several months. Your definition may have some of the same elements. Yours may have more to it or less, but the foundation must be there for us to experience the true definition of Love. What is LOVE? Love is...

CHAPTER TWO

Microwavable Minute Rice

Complete Commitment

*T*here it was, Kroger grocery store, aisle nine, top shelf. I wasn't looking for it, but it caught my eye for some reason. It was the perfect example of our society: Microwavable Minute Rice. Why did it catch my eye? It's just ironic that Minute Rice is no longer quick enough. Sixty seconds is now just too long to wait. We now need Microwavable Minute Rice!

Our society is an instant gratification society, an "I want what I want, when I want it, and how I want it" society. One of the main problems with most relationships today is that they don't meet this demand of instant perfection and are conveniently brushed aside. The large and growing majority of people today consciously live by this creed. The danger lies in the expectation of perfection without knowledge of how to truly love and care for the other person in the relationship. Possibly the most important element of Love is commitment, the opposite of this trend.

I often thought I wanted romance or the rush of feelings to be the center of a relationship, but I quickly found that those subjective aspects make a poor, shallow, and weak foundation. We must start with commitment, build on commitment, and constantly revisit commitment if there is to be any long term success in a relationship. Scott Peck's book, <u>*A Road Less Traveled*</u>, puts it beautifully. He shares the concept that the end of romantic love is not the end of love at all; rather it is the beginning of genuine love. Where feelings fade, commitment continues.[1]

We have too often tied the emotions involved with our natural hormonal reaction to the idea of love! The truth is that real love is defined quite differently. We will begin to discover love really is based on a conscious decision of the will rather than a fleeting feeling that may not decide to show up or stick around. The great part is when we do find that special someone who makes our heart flutter, and we make his or hers pound, and we agree to commit to each other. Please do not stop with the idea that love is only a commitment. Don't go out searching for someone who will simply put up with you and commit your life to them. Wrong! Love is first a commitment.

My friends Eddie and Mandy are a great example. They were sharing some stories with me about their first born, Jonathan.

I doubt seriously they would recount this particular event if I were to ask them to name the most loving memory of their son.

Their son Jonathan was screaming late one night. They went to his room only to find he had vomited everywhere. (It gets even worse.) Eddie and Mandy had to clean him up, wash his bed, and give him a bath because it was everywhere; the memory is such a precious one. They then had to shower and change because he had gotten all over them as well. Finally, they got back to bed around 5:00 and had to get up at 6:00. They would not share this encounter with the romance and warmth we normally associate with love, but isn't that what love is? Real love. It doesn't sound good, or feel good, or smell good, yet we meet the needs of someone dear to us. Where the feelings stop real love starts. Where the feelings stop commitment reveals itself.

A biblical example is found in Luke 22:42. Jesus is in the garden praying the night before He was to be crucified. The only man to ever have perfect love expresses the entire concept of love being first and foremost a commitment. He asked the Father, "If you are willing, take this cup from me." With anguish that caused him to sweat blood, he begged this would not have to take place. Separation from the Father did not feel good or sound good, and it would be more painful than anything we will ever know. Yet, Jesus' commitment was so vivid when He proclaimed to the Father, "not my will, but yours be done."

This passage illustrated to me clearly that love is a commitment, not a feeling. But, we can't stop with commitment alone. It is the foundation and is vital, but is not the only element. I can envision some super-spiritual person seeking out the most rude person possible and committing to him or her for the sake of finding love. Truth be known, at times we are all difficult to live with.

When we do find ourselves in a relationship, there will certainly be times that we'll think we are with the most difficult person on the earth; sometimes they may feel the same. That is why commitment is imperative in every phase. My mentor for several years gave me a great piece of advice with regard to commitment in a relationship. "When you fall in love, date a woman through the seasons; then you will know if you are ready to commit your life." Commitment is the key element no matter what stage you are in.

My search for improving my relationships started with defining love. God began to prompt my heart asking me if I wanted to be in love. I responded, "Of course I do!" He asked me again, and the response I gave was an even more emphatic, "YES!"

After the question continued to pop into my mind again and again, I finally realized my answer was amiss. The question could not be answered with what I said, thought, agreed with, argued, felt or aspired to do. The answer became clear and simple in the form of a question. I had to ask myself, "Am I committed to passionately pursuing what love really is? Will I focus my life on becoming what I find? Will I embody the qualities that are synonymous with God's definition of love?"

Reality is that what I study, ponder, articulate, discover, and even agree with mean next to nothing. The question you and I must answer if we are to find real love is, "Are we willing to commit to finding out the truth and diligently apply it in our lives?" So many people I meet take the absentee approach to the problem. It would be like complaining about the current politicians, but never exercising the right to vote. Multiply that and personalize it.

Countless people try to bolster areas in their lives that are good and expect their relationships to benefit. I am personally guilty of this. It is too easy to sit back and say, "I love God, and I am doing fine in these other areas of my life. So it's all those women out there who have the problem." I would venture to say that many women feel the same way toward men.

No aspect of our personal relationship with God is dependent on someone else to start, especially commitment. The journey to being in a loving relationship starts in our own hearts regardless of our current situation. Are you ready to start the journey? If so, take a look at how God defines love. Read the following passages and consider these truths carefully.

1. Character of Love Philippians 4:8
2. Process of Love II Peter 1:5-7
3. Definition of Love I Corinthians 13:4-7

Now ask the question,"What qualities do I need to work on?" You may want to pray and ask God to show you where to start. When I asked, God simply said, "Pick one. You need work in all of them." He was right, and I still do.

Commitment is vital. We must be individually committed to putting what God says about love into action. How do we put these truths into action if we are not involved with someone? What areas of life are we committed to? The second element of love answers that question and lies just ahead.

¹ Peck, Scott. <u>A Road Less Traveled</u>
(New York, New York. Touchstone, 1980,1998)

CHAPTER THREE

Sharing Tongues

Getting Real

I'm sure some readers have turned right to this chapter before reading anything else because of the catchy title. Some may think, "This is the part about relationships I really want to know about!" In an odd sort of way this could very well be the most important part of the Love definition. Allow me to briefly explain before we go straight to sharing tongues.

In Matthew 22:37,39, Jesus is asked to name the greatest commandment. He states clearly and concisely, "Love the Lord your God with all your heart, and with all your soul, and with all your mind." Jesus adds, "Love your neighbor as yourself." This condensed version of the entire Bible is a wonderful outline for the second element of our Love definition. It also answers the questions, "Where and how do I make a complete commitment to His truth in our relationship with Him and with others?" You may feel that it sounds much too simple. Not really!

People have become so overcome with their religion that they don't even know what they are saying and doing. To love God with all your heart, soul, and strength is not a religious agreement to attend Sunday school more often, sing in the choir, or tithe more faithfully. Those are certainly great disciplines, but loving is simply getting real, or being genuine and honest, with God on a very personal level.

One church in Florida has obviously missed this concept of being real as have many of us. I noticed this as I was on tour in the Sunshine State and driving with some friends to dinner. The radio played a well-meaning commercial from a local church proclaiming their benefits. They actually said, "Come to our church. We believe in sharing tongues!" Now I don't know about your worship preference, but when I go to church I don't care to share my tongue with anyone.

I had this bizarre picture in my mind of an usher at the door, handing out bulletins and greeting people with a holy kiss that was much more than scripture intended. They should have advertised on their marquee, "Please brush and floss before all services." To love God with all our heart is not to see how pious we can appear or how religious we can sound. Until we experience a relationship with God, we will not be ready to fully enjoy any other relationship.

God longs for us to get real with Him because of how special we are to him. Two of my favorite verses in all of the Bible are found in Psalms 139. Before we look at the verses, use your imagination for a minute. Picture yourself relaxing at the beach on a hot summer day. There is a gentle breeze coming off the water. The waves are crashing in the distance and you just sat down on your towel to dry off from a swim. Now take up a handful of sand. How many grains can you hold in your hand? Now look as far as you can up and down the beach. How many grains of sand can you see on the entire beach? Close your eyes and picture it. Millions... billions... trillions?

Yet in Ps. 139:17-18, David is getting real with God with all his heart and writes, "How precious to me are your thoughts, Oh God! How vast is the sum of them! Were I to count them, they would outnumber the grains of sand." Jeremiah 29:11-12, says, "I know the plans I have for you, declares the Lord, plans to prosper you and not to harm you, plans to give you hope and a future. Then you will call upon me and come and pray to me, and I will listen to you." If there is one thing we must grasp, it is God's overwhelming desire to provide our every need with His resources.

In addition to knowing a real God who cared enough to listen to my needs, my personal relationships needed a major dose of hopefulness for the future. It wasn't until I began to live like this was true that my relationships began to improve. We must get personal with God! We are admonished in I Peter 5:7 to cast all our anxieties upon Him because He cares for us. God and God alone can meet our needs, ease our fears, and fully understand our concerns.

It is time we fall hopelessly at His feet giving Him control of our lives, specifically our relationships, and put our hope and trust in Him. If you have never taken the time to pour out your heart to God, do it now. Become honest with Him. I had to get rid of a religious facade and tell God I was hurt, disappointed, and lonely. I also had to ask why it appeared He wasn't doing anything to help. That effort toward honesty opened the flood gates of insight. If we are to move forward, we must first come with a genuine heart to the Lord.

New Christians are probably best at getting real. They haven't had time to learn how to fake it. My favorite prayer of all time is from a few years back. It was straightforward and simple. I was traveling with a church on a ski retreat, driving in vans for six hours. Tired and starving upon arrival, we entered the only place in town still open – pizza!! (my favorite food on the planet). The wait staff began putting the modern day manna on the tables, and one of the starved students asked who would do the blessing. Finally, Mike, a new believer, spoke up and said, "I'll do it."

After a brief pause for the taking off of hats and grabbing of hands, it happened. From the bottom of his heart Mike prayed, "God we love pizza. Thanks!" That was it! I wish we could have seen our Heavenly Father physically. I am certain He was standing right there going, "Cool! I know you do!! Eat it!"

A pastor friend up north recounted a similar situation one night in his church. A recent convert was sitting on the front pew during the service. Very excited about his new freedom and filled with joy, he was a sight to see. The church did not know what was about to happen. The final prayer was spoken and the pastor in traditional form prompted the congregation with, "And all God's people said..." But before anyone could grunt the usual response, "Amen," this excited new brother yelled, "ALL RIGHT!" Three deacons fainted. This pastor shared with me that since then they close every Sunday evening service with the proclamation, "And all God's people said, ALL RIGHT!"

Jesus said, "Let the little ones come to me. Do not hinder them. The kingdom of God belongs to such as these."[1] We will not experience true love until we have come to be transparent and completely real before the all knowing, completely loving God. You never have to wonder what children are thinking or feeling. They wear it on their sleeves. God is demanding the same of us in our relationship with Him if we are to discover the true love He has in store for us. We cannot give something to others that we have never received. God longs to give us the love we so desperately long for and need.

Once we have allowed God to give such a love to us we are then free to fulfill the second great command –"Love your neighbor as yourself."[2] People long to know someone with nothing to hide. I have done an unofficial survey among various groups of singles, business people, church members, bus drivers, fast food employees, and many more. Thousands of people when asked what they look for most in someone of the opposite sex replied with something similar to 'someone who is real'. What you see is what you get. Isn't that interesting? Not money, not fame, not looks, but someone who is genuine.

My mentor taught me a key lesson in looking for the genuine person. "When you fall in love and are ready to get married wait... wait until she burps in front of you." I thought about it for a minute. Wait until she burps? Could you show me the verse that says that? I imagined falling in love, dating, and wanting to get married. I'd go buy the ring, put it in the glove compartment of my car, and take her out for Mexican food every night for a week. She would finally break. BURP!

"Oh, excuse me," she'd say with an embarrassed tone. I'd quickly open the prize door, pull out the ring, and ask her to marry me. Can you imagine what she would say to her friends when they asked how I proposed?

Al, my mentor, told me that until she burps in front of you, you haven't seen all of her. Now ladies, I do not suggest this as an opening line, "Hi I'm Judy. . . BURP!" But there is some serious merit to the idea of getting real. The thought that God made us each unique is not hard to swallow. It is the freedom to become that person that is scary. We are all different. God used my several roommates to prove this point and bless me with the situations to grow in this element. One such insight happened in the last place I lived before I was married.

I am a night person by nature. I can go very late into the night and not even think about it. If you are not sure if you are a night or a morning person try to find yourself in this situation. I happen to sleep strangely. My head rests on a pillow, a pillow is on top of my head, and I have one to hug in front. It doesn't matter if I have gotten ten hours of sleep when that alarm clock starts blaring, I start swinging. BAM! (snooze bar). Those extra ten minutes are the most important ten minutes in my life. A question for all you night people. Do you ever set the alarm twenty or thirty minutes early just so you can hit it two or three times? It feels like we have control and are cheating time.

The first morning in this new bachelor pad I hit my alarm and out of nowhere came this music. I hit the clock several times but it wouldn't stop. It was coming from downstairs. I grappled my way out of bed and started down stairs to find the source of this obnoxious noise.

At this point you have to imagine what I look like at 6:00 AM Yes, 6:00 AM. This is news for many night people that 6:00 comes twice in the same day. I look bad at 6:00AM. I usually have on my old boxers and my torn up T-shirt. Because of my pillow, I have this mutation of a Mohawk on my head. My face looks as if someone took a red ink pen and wrote directions to his house on my cheek. Then there is that crusty drool spot in the corner of my mouth. It may sound gross, but remember this is about being real, and I know you too have drooled at sometime. It is in this condition I confront the source of this invasion of my right to quiet. There he was standing in the kitchen. I asked in a frustrated voice, "What are you doing?"

Standing there perfectly dressed in a suit holding a cup of coffee, my roomate replied with a smirk on his face, "Oh, you've obviously never roomed with a morning person who likes to sing, ha, ha, ha..." I broke the humor with a self divulging of my own. "Well you must have never roomed with an ax murderer before, so shut up!"

You may be different. You may actually like to pop out of bed ten minutes before the alarm goes off and go for your three mile jog. Then you energetically come home and do your Abs of Steel video and take a nice cold shower to freshen up. If the later of the two descriptions is you, then you are not a night person. You are a ...sick person, and need to get some serious help. Don't get me wrong. I like morning people. I like to keep them up past 10:00PM and watch them wilt. Do you get the picture? People are very different.

Now think of all the other variables involved. Different interest, skills, gifts, talents, personalities, temperaments, and the list goes on and on. Then add in God's greatest prompt for humor: Men and Women. It may have gone something like this, "I need a good laugh this millennium," God said. "I have a great idea; I'll make them male and female!"

The rest is history. Men and women start out different and become even more unique. My wife teaches middle school and loves it. I have visited her school a few times and other then the clothing styles, little has changed. Lunch time was and still is my favorite for observing male and female differences. See if you remember.

Boys finish their meal and take a piece of paper. Each folds it up into a triangle that is a what? ...A football, right! (As young men we could sit for hours grunting back and forth) "Uh, uh, uh, yah... Touchdown!!" Then they place the fingers into the shape of a miniature goal post and have a friend flick a tri-pointed object at another's face. This ritual has been repeated for generations all over the country.

The only thing more popular than football is what girls do with the same piece of paper at the same time. Their paper folding creation is much more involved and carries meaning that is vital to life as we know it. Girls spend ten times longer making their origami love connection tools.

After completion they converge and converse. Placing four fingers into this paper computer, they predict the rest of your life. A carefully selected number is given, then the shoe size, eye color, and favorite color are told to the group. Then cautiously they open a section of the paper and proclaim with great confidence, "Okay, you are going to live in the suburbs, marry Fred, have two kids, a ranch style house, drive a Volvo, and have a dog named Binky." All from this paper thing. The differences between men and women continue to grow with time.

How are you different? What makes you tick? Take a minute and get honest with God. What do you like about yourself? Relax. It's okay. You are most likely alone and not reading this with someone over your shoulder. Thank God for the things you like about yourself.

Make a list of the talents you feel God has given you. Have some fun; list the personality traits you think you possess. What is your best quality? Now list the things you wish were different. If they need to be confessed as past failures, do so.

One of my absolute favorite characteristics of God is His ability to forgive and forget. He chooses to forgive, so you and I can too. Being honest is taking the good and bad and putting it all at His feet. Once we have done that we can be free to be all He intended us to be, free to perform the ultimate gift of love. The final element of the definition. **Love is a complete commitment to getting real**, but there is one more vital element.

[1]Matthew 19:14
[2]Matthew 22:39

CHAPTER FOUR

I Just Wanted To Be With You

Giving Unconditionally

I was in the final phase of my dating life with Heather (now my wife). We were at a couple's house who have been married for ten years and are still going strong. They asked the often awkward question, "So how are you two doing?" They were not asking about our general well being, rather the tone had a 'How serious are you two?' quality. It wasn't an uncomfortable question because we had talked recently and we agreed that marriage was in our future.

With this in mind, I asked our married friends to explain why we should get married. My friend Stan with his quick wit said simply, "You're a Christian, so living together is out of the question."

I agreed, of course, then followed with asking him the main reasons to get married. Stan, in only a bit more serious tone responded, "Well if you can't figure out the first reason you may have the gift of singleness."

I shared with great confidence that I did not have that gift. When I asked for other reasons to embark on such a committed life, to my surprise he came up with the most insightful element I had ever heard.

I began to see marriage in a whole new light. His answer has continued to give me hope and direction in how I can and should be treating my wife. It is like a light came on and I said, "Yeah, that's why marriage is set up this way. That's why complete commitment is important. That's why God thought of this in the first place." Do you want to know what he said?

Stan said, "If you are looking for someone to meet your needs, make you happy, and make your life worthwhile, you will be greatly disappointed, quickly discouraged, and basically unhappy the rest of your life. But, if you will just be the person God has made you to be, and find out how you can give your life to someone else by meeting her needs and making her happy, you will discover fulfillment, joy, and peace in ways you can't even imagine."

WOW! It made sense. The next morning I had a great time with the Lord during my Bible reflections and ended up studying what is probably the most popular verse in modern times. It was the ninth word of John 3:16. I couldn't get out of my head. *"For God so loved the world that He **gave** his only Son..."* (Emphasis added). Love is certainly a complete commitment. Love is definitely getting real with God and others. This element of giving just brings it all together. God so loved, He gave.

Success in life is not in what we get, it is in what we give. Things we obtain, power we possess, fame we achieve will never fill that lasting need we can only find in giving. Those things are temporary and there will always seem to be a need for more. When we receive something, the pleasure is for the moment and then gone forever. Giving has the opposite effect. Jesus said in Acts 20:35, "It is more blessed to give than to receive." Why?

Actually, I am not sure why, but I am discovering this is a definite fundamental truth. My greatest joys in life can be traced to times of giving. Seldom does notoriety or an object even come close to truly fulfilling our needs. It is when God chooses to use a mere human to touch a heart or meet a need that a true, lasting abundant life is discovered.

Once we allow God to give us His provision for sin, His plan for life, and His power to live it, we cannot help but want to give it away. However, we must have something to give. Understanding His complete love is paramount. The only condition to His love is our acceptance. It truly is a gift waiting for you and me to open and experience fully. I have believed this truth since inviting Christ into my heart, but not until a few years ago did God paint such a vivid picture to me of His love for us.

Fall in the Tennessee mountains was breathtaking. The leaves were brilliant; the Pigeon River deep and roaring. I sat on a rock that jutted out over the water. Dangling my feet over the edge, I reviewed my notes for the college student retreat that day. Most of all I was soaking in the colors and the crisp mountain air.

Then out of the corner of my eye something caught my attention. Walking dangerously close to the edge of the water was a little girl. She could not have been more than about four years old, and she was alone. Afraid she was going to slip off the bank and be swept away by the rushing water, I quickly got up and motioned her away from the water.

I approached the little adventurer and said, "Hi, what's your name? She quickly shot back, "What's your name?" ignoring my question.

I responded, "Well, I'm Kenn. What are you doing down here?"

She quizzed, "What are you doing down here?" in her new-found pattern of responses.

To avoid having to answer yet another of my own questions, I decided to try a new approach. "I'm skipping rocks! Would you like to try?"

She didn't utter a word, but following a bold affirmative nod we were skipping rocks. While throwing I prodded for some general information. "Are your parents here? Do they know you are down here? Are they up in the cabin?"

This cute little face, focused on the new discipline of making the rocks hop, shook up and down with intermittent yet affirming grunts. I was able to decipher that her parents were indeed in the cabin above but probably did not know where she was. I suggested we skip a few more rocks then go let her parents know where we were. This seemed acceptable, and we were soon on the path up to the cabin.

It turned out that she was the associate pastor's youngest daughter, Tommi. She was four years old and had curly, bleached blonde hair, brown eyes, and loads of energy. That little bit of time she and I spent together made more of an impact on both of us than I had realized.

The day at the retreat went well, and all the sessions had gone successfully. That night would leave an indelible mark on my heart. After the final group time, I found a couch in the great room of the cabin where I was staying. The students were mingling as the fire roared. The night was cool, and a productive fatigue was quickly overtaking me.

A group of students in front of me began to part. I noticed it was Tommi making her way through the crowd. She cleared through the students and walked over to the couch where I was sitting. Without a greeting she calmly climbed up on the sofa, sat right next to me, scooted over to my hip, and nuzzled her shoulder under my outstretched arm. (Now, females did not normally approach me in this way.) Shocked and flattered, I greeted my new friend and asked, "Hi, what do you want?"

She stared at me with those big brown eyes and with a coy smile said in a shy voice, "I just wanted to be with you." Words cannot describe what happened to my heart. Where it came from I do not know. I was overcome with a flood of emotion and the sudden urge to give her my wallet, and my keys, and my money. I was thinking, "Here take it all, whatever you want."

The next day while driving to Nashville, I could not get this feeling out of my mind. I hate to use the word feeling because it was so much more than that. I prayed, "God, I am going to make the worst father in the world. She wasn't even my little girl. All she did was sit with me and I was ready to give her everything."

God has never spoken to me audibly, but this small voice in my heart was unmistakable. God moved on my heart and said, "Kenn you're going to be okay. I just wanted you to know how I feel about you every day." I will never forget that sense of complete acceptance. God longs only to give us all that is good. His love is contagious. When we truly understand it we will never be the same. We must give it away.

UNDERSTANDING
Love

CHAPTER FIVE

Big Macs And Vitamins

Fundamental vs. Supplemental Needs

*S*ixth grade was a confusing and exciting time. Changing classes for the first time, getting a locker, wearing cool clothes (well, we thought they were cool at the time), and discovering that girls were no longer gross. Sixth grade was my first real encounter with love. Looking back from any point in life, the previous stage always seems easier doesn't it? Junior high certainly seemed easy for me as I think back. I doubt the standard procedure has changed much since the invention of the writing utensil.

Three weeks into the first quarter I received my first love note. Prompted by one cute sixth grader, but written and delivered by her best friend. The note read something like:

Kenny,
Neia likes you. Do you like her?
　　　YES or No
　　　(Circle one)

Girls knew they needed to write out, "Circle one" or the guy would stand there for hours trying to figure out what to do next. Love sure was simple then. I circled my response, and before I knew it, we were going together. I am not sure where we went, but for three glorious days we went together. We swapped name bracelets and it was the most…different time of my life. I must not have gone together correctly or something because I soon received another note saying Neia did not want to go with me anymore. Oh, yes, and to give back her bracelet.

The grown up version of this is a crossroad I have come to know as The TALK. Notes seemed so much easier but, women decided somewhere down the road to change venues. After being dumped more than once you can almost tell when the TALK is coming. I know this only because of my superior intelligence, vast experience, and the fact that the TALK was always initiated by the girls saying, "We need to TALK."

They would always say something like, "Kenn, you are so wonderful, handsome and kind. You'll make a wonderful father. You are everything a girl looks for and more. You're just perfect.

That is why I think we should...date other people...but I still want to be friends." All I could think of was, "Where do I circle?"

FUNDAMENTAL INTIMACY SOURCE

So why do we subject ourselves to this cycle of hope and hurt, exhilaration and exasperation? Where does the desire to keep going back time and time again come from?

It comes from the way we are made. God designed us with a natural need for intimacy. The problem is that we do not take the time to find the right intimacy to meet the right need. Most failure and frustration comes from a misunderstanding about the types of and the need for intimacy. As Bill Hybles in his book, _Fit To Be Tied_, puts it so beautifully, "Perhaps we fail to understand that God created human beings to yearn for **two levels of relational intimacy**. The first level can be met by establishing a deep, honest, trusting relationship with a friend or marriage partner. The second level can only be met by entering into an authentic, growing relationship with God."[1] (Emphasis added.)

The most important or fundamental intimacy need we have has very little, if anything, to do with relationships with the opposite sex. Jesus did not say in John 10:10, "I came that they may have life and have it abundantly..."[2] Oh yes, but only once they get married. Abundant life is not contingent on marriage or even on getting a date. The abundant life, (hope, peace, joy, fulfillment, happiness), is contingent on only one type of intimacy. Fundamental intimacy. People have tried throughout time to fill this fundamental need with supplemental sources and it never works.

Money, power, marriage, sex, drugs, fame... nothing can fill the fundamental need for intimacy except the fundamental source. That fundamental source is a personal relationship with God.

Although God has done all the work to provide the opportunity for a relationship, it is clear we as individuals make that choice to start and establish the relationship. In Rev. 3:20, Jesus says to you and me, "Behold, I stand at the door and knock. If any one hears my voice and opens the door I will come in..."

Several pastors have made the observation that the only door knob is on the inside, and only we can open that door. Finding the source to meet our fundamental intimacy need is as easy as opening that door. The process is laid out for whosoever, anybody (John 3:16). When we agree with God that we have sinned and fall short of being perfect, (Romans 3:23), we have taken the first step. When we accept that Jesus took the punishment for that sin and imperfection (Romans 6:23) we have taken the second step. The decisive step, though, is when we of our own will choose to believe that Jesus is the only forgiveness for our sin (John 14:6) and that we place our hope and trust in Him. We invite Him into our lives to forgive our imperfections and direct our lives. (1 John 5:11-13). The fundamental intimacy source begins to fill the fundamental intimacy need. Yes, I said begins to fill.

Are we complete in Christ when we invite Him into our lives? YES! Yet, we must establish this source as our fundamental supply. Too many Christians (me included) for too long have the complete, perfect **fundamental** source yet keep looking to **supplemental** supplies to meet this need.

Let's move from the theoretical into hard reality. There is an overwhelming attitude among many Christians today of, "Once I invite Christ into my life, I can do things the way I think or feel they should be done, pray about them, and God should bless me." It would be like me as a child saying to my earthly father, "I accept the fact that you are my Dad. I will now do things my way and you should bless me." My way was often greeted with the blessing of a spanking, discipline, and time in my room to ponder who was in control. Our heavenly Father is infinitely wise and He knows what is going to meet our needs.

Prayer is not a vending machine nor is God a brainless genie. The way we experience God meeting our fundamental needs, providing peace, directing us to hope, and finding us the path to fulfillment is by individually establishing that fundamental supply. In plain English, doing it His way or not at all.

For too long I had thought that since I am a Christian and God is forgiving, loving, and gracious that I could do what I thought was right and He would bless or forgive my actions and everything just worked out, right? God is gracious, loving, and understanding and does... "work all thing together for our good..." (Romans 8:28) But don't miss the end of this verse, "... to those who love God and are called according to His purpose."

We must allow God to provide the fundamental intimacy in our lives and direct us according to His plan. The way we do this is by committing in our hearts to pursue relationships according to His purpose or not at all. We will not always understand His way, yet we must choose to follow it. His way will not always feel natural, but we must choose His way anyway. It may not be the popular way, but we must choose to trust it.

As dedicated sons and daughters, we must stop sprinkling religious words and deeds on our self conceived ideas expecting them to meet our fundamental intimacy needs. Another major fault I am guilty of is expecting his blessing on my relationships due to obedience to His will in other areas of my life. This attitude is wrong. As Galatians 6:7 simply states, whatever we sow, we will reap. Therefore, we must plant the right seeds in every area of our lives.

If we are not experiencing the fundamental intimacy need being met in our lives, then we either don't have the proper relationship to start with, or we are not establishing it in the relationship area of our lives. Establishing the trust in Him as the fundamental need source is vital to our relational success.

Even at the ripe old age of seven I wanted to be successful in everything I did. At that age football was much more important to me than relationships, though. When I look back it is clear the faithfulness of God was there to teach me this truth even then.

The Smyrna Jets needed a linebacker, and this sixty-five pound boy was it. The pads were bigger than I was, but at that age it was so cool to wear the uniform and act like the big guys. Football was not big in our family yet my Dad was still very supportive. Each week he would sit up on the grassy bank next to the field and watch the games. On the way home from each game we would talk about many issues related to football but mostly about how I played. Two games in particular stick out in my mind from that year.

One week in the middle of the season we had won big. Four touchdowns! After the game I could not wait to hear my dad's reaction to the skill and effort of the outside linebacker more commonly know as Kenny. We rehashed the game and the five or six tackles I made. As we drove into the neighborhood my Dad made a closing comment that stuck with me. "You played a great game, but do you remember the play in the last quarter when you were winning by five touchdowns? The one where they ran a reverse with two and a half minutes left?"

I shrugged it off with a, "Yeah, he was gone by a mile and we were going to win anyway. It didn't matter."

"Yeah, it does matter," my Dad gently but firmly injected. "You never know what can happen. He could have stumbled, or fallen, or fumbled, and you need to be there to make every play you can. **You never give up**. They could have scored and gotten a couple on-side kicks." At that age I believed everything my Dad said, and in Pee-Wee football anything can happen. "Play until you hear the whistle. Never give up. You played a good game."

I did not think another thing about it. I recounted my great plays to my Mom and was bigger than life for a week. The next week was not so great. Instead of leading by five touchdowns, we were losing by four touchdowns, down 24 points (little guys don't often make extra points). Worse, it was raining and it was about forty degrees. This was not fun.

With less than a minute left, the other team ran a sweep to the opposite side and my team was not too intent on stopping them. What did it matter? Lose by 24 points or 30, who cares? Their tail back was twenty yards ahead of everyone. Then this voice in my helmet started going off. Play till the whistle, NEVER GIVE UP! I took off with the ultimate of optimism. I'll catch him, he'll fumble, I'll run it back, touchdown, on-side kick, we could still win..."

As the rain beat down and the cold gripped me, I realized everyone else on the field quit running except the guy with the ball and me. As we trounced trough the puddles and mud, he slowed up a little. I closed the gap from fifteen yards, to ten yards, to five yards, his jersey was right at my fingertips...

Now, this would be a great story... if I had caught the guy. If he had fumbled and I had the chance to score it would have been such a wonderful example. He did not fumble. All I caught was a cold. I was wet and cold, and now exhausted. The final horn sounded and we lost by five touchdowns. Frustrated, wet, dejected, and a little mad, I made my way up the grassy hill, took off my shoulder pads, soaked and muddy, I climbed into our Plymouth Valiant, my chin on my chest and my lower lip puffed out.

Dad got into the car. Without pausing he said, "You played a great game!"

Wondering if he had watched my game, I said, " What?" I didn't lift my head and I was about to cry from embarrassment.

"That last play," he said.

In a minor fit of anger I said with my head buried, "He didn't fumble, I didn't catch him, and we lost!"

"That doesn't matter," he said with a proud grin. "He scored but you didn't give up! I was so proud of you!"

For the first time I looked out the window and I noticed we weren't going home. Where are we going? McDonalds! (I lit up like a Christmas tree.) When we arrived the surprise got even better. My Dad, who was very tight with money, shocked me. My sister, brother and I never got to order anything but what kind of drink we wanted. It was always a small hamburger, small fries, then we could pick a small Coke or Sprite.

But, not this trip. The young lady asked for our order. My dad turned to me and said, "Go ahead." In shock I asked him what he meant. He said, "Anything you want." Wow! I could get a Big Mac, no, I want two Big Macs, large fry, large Coke, large chocolate milk shake. Seven years old and sixty-five pounds – I sat there with a Big Mac in each hand.

The game long forgotten and all I could think about was, "I DIDN'T GIVE UP! No one will likely ever remember that the Vikings beat the Jets in Smyrna that day, but I learned something that I will never forget.

God longs to teach us in the same way. Our relationships can be unforgettably great when we choose to establish God and His way as the fundamental source for all our needs. We must commit to having relationships with the opposite sex His way or not at all.

SUPPLEMENTAL INTIMACY SOURCE

I love my wife Heather more than golf. I love her more than Ben & Jerry's Chocolate Chip Cookie Dough Ice Cream. I love my wife more than breathing. I love her more than food. Okay, you get the idea. As much as I love her and would do anything for her, I cannot now nor will I ever be able to compete with God. He is just too awesome. He can use absolutes you and I can only talk about. He can say things like "...surely I am with you **always**..." (Matthew 28:20) and, "**Never** will I leave you..." (Hebrews 13:5).[1] He can back up each statement. How can we compete with that?

You may be saying to that absurd question, "Kenn you have lost it; of course we cannot compete with that." But, how many of us try? How many of us expect another human to meet the fundamental needs only God can? Numerous relationships and marriages tragically fail for this very reason. A wife looks for her husband to meet her fundamental need for security. A husband looks for his wife to meet his fundamental need for significance. These are pressures to meet a need that God and God alone can satisfy. It is only when we realize that another person cannot and will not make us totally happy, bring us complete joy, provide us with lasting peace, and give constant fulfill-ment that we begin to discover relationships the way God made them.

From the very beginning we see that God designed men and women to be a supplemental intimacy source to meet supplemental intimacy needs. In Genesis chapter two we find Adam rooting around the garden. He is making it happen. He is naming animals, growing food, digging a garden within the garden.

Imagine Adam on his knees trenching trough the dirt with a rock. Dig, dig, grunt, grunt. The garden is happening and is fundamentally fine. Then comes verse 18 and God says, "It is not good for the man to be alone, I will make him a helper..." God was probably thinking, "Hey, Adam is going to ignore the directions or go walking and get lost. Look, he is digging with a rock..."

Enter the helper suitable for him. Eve quietly stands next to Adam and says, "Here, try this shovel!" Adam grabs it and starts digging away with much more success.

Notice that our friend Adam was getting it done. All the fundamental needs met. Eve came along to simply make it better. But, if we look to that supplemental source to meet our fundamental needs, look out. Adam knew the source for all his needs. When he listened to the supplemental source, Eve, to meet a fundamental need, Wisdom and Knowledge, there was trouble. Adam is thinking the shovel was a good idea. Why not trust the helper God gave me instead of God? Have an apple? Okay. Wrong!

A supplemental source was never meant to meet a fundamental need. It is important in relationships to never put the expectations and pressures on anyone to meet our fundamental needs. The relationship can only result in failure. Supplemental vitamins are good if they are taken in conjunction with a well balanced diet. It does not matter how great the vitamins are if there is no food in the diet. The reason so many relationships burn hot and then burn out is that they are relying on the supplemental source to fill that fundamental need, and eventually the relationship will die of malnutrition. It cannot last.

Allow me to paint a very clear picture of how this truth should look in the reality of relationships. Philippians 4:4-5 says "Rejoice in the Lord always, again: Rejoice! Let your gentle spirit be known to men the Lord is near."[3] We should be so fundamentally 'full' that we can walk into every type of social situation this way. Happiness is the result because we do not need anything—we already have it all.

No one can make us happy. We are already happy. You cannot bring someone complete peace when he or she already has it. Joy? Already got it. Purpose? Got it. The only things not brought to the party are an agenda and expectations. You cannot lose with this person. He expects nothing from you, so anything is a bonus for you. The best anyone can do is help you and me be more of what we already are. God has met all our needs. Phillipians 4:6 says that if I do have any needs to take them to the fundamental source, and He will take care of them.

The greatest part of understanding this truth is in verse seven. When we trust Him to meet our fundamental needs, He makes us a promise that anyone who has ever been dumped needs to hear and hold on to. Trust Him and He will give you and me peace that surpasses comprehension, that will guard our hearts and minds. We won't get hurt or make stupid mistakes. Believe me, it works and if you want to avoid making the same mistakes over and over, establish God as your source to meet your fundamental needs. His peace and protection are worth it.

[1]Hybels, Bill. *Fit To Be Tied*
(Grand Rapids, MI: Zondervan Pub. House, 1991), p.32.

[2]New American Standard (Here after referred to NAS)
(Chicago, IL. Moody Press, 1995)

[3]NAS

CHAPTER SIX

Road Map To Love

*Defining And Becoming
The Character Of Love*

*D*ream big. In Psalms 37:4 we see that if we delight in the Lord He will give us the desires of our hearts. Ephesians 3:20 states that God is able to do more than we can ask for or dream. What ever happened to the idea that dreams come true? It certainly was not God's idea to quit dreaming. Too many think that the handsome, nurturing, romantic man or the beautiful, smart, supportive woman will have to exist only in fantasy.

Our dreams have been replaced with the harsh reality of compromise, failure, loss of hope, and lack of faith. What occurs many times is that reality of the past pushes our dreams into a room marked unrealistic hopes. Good news: God is in the business of cleaning out rooms and making dreams a reality again.

Your prince is waiting; the princess is looking for you right now. The question is are you ready? A problem with numerous singles, and even married folks, is that we are looking to find love instead of becoming that very love we are looking for. Instead of passively sitting back and hoping fate will smile upon us and that special someone will fall into our lives, God has a much better idea. It is time we quit asking the question, "Where is my special someone?" and started asking, "**Am I going to be worth finding?**"

Contrary to popular belief God has a lot to say about finding that specific love we are searching for. He has a well detailed plan with some very detailed directions. It is our choice to take Him at His word and start moving toward the goal. We have to take the plan, follow the directions and start becoming the love we are looking for.

THE PLAN

The starting point of the PLAN is the same for everyone. Only God could come up with a plan that works no matter what your situation. If you are married, it works. If you are seriously dating, it will be a tremendous insight to see where your relationship needs to go. His Plan gives such clarity for those who are trying to decide what dating is all about. And for those of you that are in the same boat I was, dateless and clueless, discovering this plan was a catalyst for great hope and purpose. So what exactly is this PLAN?

Before we look at the plan specifically I want to give a bit of guidance. Look at this plan in three different lights. How intently you look at these different questions will depend on where you are in the relationship spectrum.

1) Ask, do *I* embody the qualities of this plan?

2) Does **the person** I am interested in or the people I invest my time with strive to embody these qualities?

3) When, or if, you are involved with someone, ask the question, does **our** relationship embody these qualities?

I have seen many times two wonderful people follow the plan on their own and ruin a great relationship by not following the plan together.

So, what is this plan?

The plan is found in Philippians 4:8-9. But before it is revealed let me make one last endorsement. Without exception, every time I have failed at a relationship or have been hurt I can draw a direct line to violating one or more of these qualities. However, every successful relationship I have ever come across had these qualities within the individuals as well as the relationship itself.

The plan is that we would seek to know and embody the character qualities needed to make relationships all that God intended them to be. Specifically:

"Finally brethren, whatever is true, whatever is honorable, whatever is right, whatever is pure, whatever is lovely, whatever is of good report, if there is any excellence and if anything worthy of praise, dwell on these things." (Phil. 4:8)

These verses go on to state that we should dwell on these qualities and practice them continually. Let's take a brief look at each to get a general idea of what it looks like. (I took one each day and spent some time dwelling on how I could better embody each quality.

Whatever is true / honest. Ask the tough questions. Do we have a tendency to tell half truths to cover ourselves? Do we exaggerate? Do we sometimes talk around issues to hide areas of our lives? God made it clear to me as I thought about being truthful in every area of my life, even recreation.

I love to play golf, but one of the toughest things to do in golf is to be honest about your score. Grown men all of a sudden have trouble counting. It is embarrassing to be the only person to be honest enough to say, yeah, I had a 13 on that hole when everyone else has rationalized their way down to a 5 or 6. We live in a society that has moved from being honest at all cost to one that encourages to be honest until it costs us, and then rationalize. When we commit ourselves to becoming the truth we have committed to the plan of becoming what God desires.

Whatever is honorable. This is a good opportunity to not only examine in ourselves, but in those we might be interested. Those who are honorable have a good track record with friends, in loyalty, trust, and confidentiality. A great question to ask with regard to someone being honorable is, "If you could not date them for some reason, would you still like them?" Honor is such a critical quality. I have seen it over and over in relationships at all levels. When feelings fail, character continues. Honor is certainly vital to God's plan.

What is right. General Norman Swartzkoff summed it up when he said, "I don't have trouble knowing what is right, my trouble comes in doing what I already know is right." Not once in my walk with the Lord have I come across a situation or a decision that I was not able to find out what was right.

What is right does not come from some super spiritual procedure. When we invite Christ into our lives He is there. When we ask Him to show us what is right with a sensitive, obedient attitude, He will. Another clue to knowing what is right is if we find ourselves wasting time trying to define what is right, instead of doing what we know has always been right, we are almost always going to be wrong. People who we can count on to do what is right in any circumstances are such a blessing. They know what God's plan is all about.

Whatever is pure. Chapter 7 will give more practical insight on purity, but let's take a quick look at two aspects. One, the Bible gives very clear directions on purity (II Tim. 2:22, Ex. 20:14, Heb. 13:4). The plan is to follow God's definition and become it. Your past may or may not be marked with impurity, but God has already dealt with your past and forgiven it. If we are to experience relationships to the fullness of His plan, we must forget what lies behind and reach forward to what lies ahead (Phil.3:13-14).

The commitment we have to make is for now and from now on to be pure. If you men are ever in question of any action being pure, let me share an idea the Lord dropped on my heart. Ask her father what he thinks is pure. That will clear up any doubts and keep the plan on track.

Whatever is lovely. This quality at first glance seems the most elusive. My friends gave me great insight on this one. Lovely is the dream. Compare yourself, your interest, and your relationships to your dream situation. Don't settle for less than God's best. My friend Stan encouraged me to marry over my head. He reminded me that we marry for life so aim high. My wife is far beyond my dreams and is the definition of lovely. I second the advice about lovely: Compare to the dream, don't settle, and marry over your head.

The final quality of the plan is *good report*. This is an easy one to start thinking about. Let's look at a couple angles. Find a few close committed friends and go over these character qualities. Ask them to rate you from 1 to 10 on each. With regard to someone you may be interested in, simply listen to those close to them. What do his or her friends say about him or her? How does he or she talk about others? Often the areas we are most critical of in others reveal the areas most needing work in our lives. Finally, what is your own report? Is it good? When talking to others do you find yourself giving good reports of your interest and the relationship, or apologizing for parts or the whole?

Please realize God's plan is much deeper and more personally intricate then we will ever be able to discover. His plan is 100% perfect for your situation and mine. The way we implement the plan is simple to understand. At the end of verse 8, Paul tells us to dwell on these things. That is exactly the first step in the plan. Take your life and situation. Pray for God to reveal the areas you need work on and how to build the qualities we just discussed. Consider each quality and I am sure you will add dozens of ideas and insights to every one of mine.

After the ideas begin to flow, it is time for the second step in implementing God's plan. Verse 9 includes the key phrase, "Practice these things." Some areas will go smoothly, others with difficulty. The promise God makes us is that He will personally be there to walk with us through it all. What a blessing! The God who shows us the way will guide us through it.

When we decide we want to pursue relationships the right way, all we have to do to begin is pick up the plan. No more waiting around hoping to one day find that nebulous love. We can start following the plan today. Building the character needed. Become the love we are looking for.

THE DIRECTIONS

Women (on average) are not good at giving directions...except to other women. The conversation usually goes something like, "Okay, you go... um, oh, I know, you go down that road..." You know THAT road? Another woman will stand there and due to the inflection or body language or some communication lacking in men will say, "Yeah! THAT road!" Then they will go on describing trees and houses and say things like, when you FEEL like you have gone too far, turn left. If women were the only ones allowed to drive we could save billions on road signs. Many women don't give great directions, but because most men don't take directions it works out fine.

Fortunately for men and women God's directions are simple, easy to understand and when we follow them, they get us to where we want to go in our relationships. The reason many people never find real love is because they don't follow directions. God's directions pick up in II Peter 1:5-9 where His plan left off.

Where we are to dwell on and practice God's plan, we are also to seek His directions by "applying all diligence." So much for sitting back and complaining about not finding the right person. The ball is in our court to get up and follow the directions. II Peter 1:5-7 gives us the directions to Love.

"Now for this very reason also, applying all diligence,
in your faith supply moral excellence, and
in your moral excellence, knowledge, and
in your knowledge, self-control, and
in your self-control, perseverance, and
in your perseverance, godliness, and
in your godliness, brotherly kindness, and
in your brotherly kindness, LOVE."

Where does the road to real love start? With moral excellence. Would you describe your life as morally excellent? If so great! I could not. (I realized I needed work on this area of my life. I would never experience the joy of Godly love.) God in His grace simply allowed me to see where I needed to start.

Any time we ask for directions the first question is usually, where are you coming from? We cannot give directions without knowing the point of origin. Some of you reading this will review these qualities and be well on your way. I encourage you at this point to not skip any of the direction. Take your time and pray through each of them. Skipping any area listed here would be as ludicrous as missing a turn and thinking, "I'll just take the next part of the directions and we will be fine." NO, you will be lost.

The flow of these qualities is there for a reason. Again, you will find much more than I ever could, but here are some starting insights. Follow along in your Bible if you would like (II Peter 1:5-7) Diligence is a must. Just reading this one time and agreeing with it won't change anything. Starting point: *Moral excellence.*DOI embody the qualities mentioned in Phil. 4:8-9? Would I describe my current view of the physical aspects of relationships as pure? Many people think they can compromise this one area and God's grace and forgiveness will just catapult them over all these required qualities and land them in love. It is not until we start following directions that we will ever experience what God has in store for us. How can I know how to live morally excellent?

Knowledge. Open up God's word and diligently find the answers. We will always move toward what we focus on. If we focus solely on our feelings and hormonal reaction, guess what? We won't become morally excellent. In II Peter 1:9 it gives the results for all who choose not to take God's directions. Those who lack these qualities become blind or short-sighted. There are numbers of blind and short sighted people out there, and I was one of them. We have to begin to see there is a direct correlation to what we choose to focus on and the results. This was never more apparent to me than after returning one weekend from a trip.

I visited my wife's parents several times before we got married. They have a very nice guest bedroom with it's own bathroom. Men occasionally read in bathrooms. I don't know where the custom started, but I feel obligated to keep up the tradition. The problem is that my in-laws only had decorating magazines in the bathroom.

I began reading the decorating magazines. (You have to read something in there.) I had no idea that those times in their restroom was having a effect on me until one Monday night. There we were in my friend's living room about to watch a football game. It was a guy's night in a guy's house. During conversation before kickoff, my mind wandered and I had an idea that I almost shared with the guys.

They stopped and said, "Did you want to say something?" I nodded that I didn't.

What I had almost blurted out in the middle of guy's night was, "Wow, this room would look really good with some window treatments and a nice chair rail border." Can you believe that? It was then that I realized what we focus on we move toward. Knowledge alone is not enough.

The writer of II Peter drives us on to realize knowledge without action does not work. We must take God's truth and practice *self-control*. Then with wisdom that could only come from experience he writes the next key, *perseverance*.

When we find the knowledge and start to apply it we will quickly discover that action goes against our nature. It takes great self-control. Even when we diligently apply self-control, there may be some bumps in the road. That is when perseverance kicks in. Perseverance is the point where we don't feel like doing the right thing any more but keep doing it anyway. This is the point where there is no turning back. We trust God despite the circumstance.

When we reach this point we begin to see *godliness*. We begin to understand. The next stage is to combat staying in this stage and proceed to – brotherly kindness. God knows what a false sense of pride can do. There are many people not experiencing love in relationships because they have chosen to stop at this point and glory in their godliness. It is much easier to look down on others than to move forward by getting down to their level.

Remember the trials and pain. There is no quality more like Jesus himself than *brotherly kindness*. There is also something magical and attractive about anyone who is willing to give while expecting nothing in return. So often I meet people who have met their spouse in the very act of serving others this way When you reach this point you won't have to look for that special someone. Love is the natural by-product.

If these directions seem a bit lofty, they are. When we seek with all diligence, trusting in Christ we will be able to effectively reach this type of love, pushing past what we are capable of on our own. Bart Starr, the former quarterback and coach of the Green Bay Packers, puts it in perspective, "Strive for perfection. Not that perfection is obtainable, but by striving for perfection we achieve excellence." God goes one better. He promises to walk with us and perfect us until Christ returns. This process showed me clearly that what we think, we do. Our actions determine our habits. Our habits define our character, and our character determines our destiny

I love the way II Peter 1:8-9 describes the results of our choosing the perfecting process. In verse 8 it says, "If these qualities are yours and are increasing, they render you neither useless nor unfruitful."[1] So we will not be useless and unfruitful. That does not seem like much of a reward for all that work. It took a while before I got the hang of this seemingly insignificant result. What I found was that when these qualities exist and increase, the natural result is being useful and fruitful. It is effortless. It is as if God is telling us to focus on the directions and He will take care of all the rest.

God's Plan and Directions can and will lead us to the type of relationships we desire.

We must discipline ourselves to embody these qualities, because it is discipline and not desire that determines destiny.

'NAS

CHAPTER SEVEN

Time To Join AAA

Constructing Relationships

*L*et's get very personal for a few pages. The truths shared to this point were prompted from circumstances in my not so successful relationship past. I was certainly tired of falling short in relationships time and time again, but that is not what pushed me over the edge. I have two records, to date, that are pretty impressive or depressing depending on your point of view. The first is that I have had eighteen roommates in my life. Many people think it is because I was a terrible roommate, but the truth is that I married off sixteen of these guys.

The other record is a bit more painful in retrospect. Of the seven women I dated seriously, six not only dumped me, but married the next guy they dated. Even with those records haunting my past, that is not what pushed me over the edge. What caused me to finally ask that tough, "What do I need to change?" question were the warning signs. As funny as these warning signs are, please remember that they actually did happen. Get out your highlighters, and if you see any of these in your life on any kind of regular basis, seek help immediately.

Warning signs that your relationship life is struggling: **1)** If you decided to sit at home on a Friday night by yourself to watch Free Willy on cable. **2)** if you have ever found yourself at K-Mart on a Saturday night with the sole purpose of buying vacuum cleaner bags. **3)** if you have ever asked a domestic pet for dating advice. **4)** I am not sure what the female equivalent is for this one, but if you men have ever been to a Disney animated movie and thought to yourself, "Wow, she is a babe!" But the big warning sign that sent me over the edge was **5)** if you are having romantic dreams each night...and you aren't in any of them.

Maybe that was a bit too personal, but we need to be open if we are to make any progress. This openness should also give you hope. If I being clueless can overcome these tragedies, certainly a normal person can.

So how does one go from experiencing some really sad warning signs to a happy relationship? Well, like I said this is the personal chapter. God began to change some areas of my life by prompting my heart in three areas: my Approach, Attitude, and Actions.

Little did I know at the time these areas needed some major reconstructing in my life. The guidelines I am about to share were also the functional tools God would use to make Galatians 5:22-23 a practical part of my relationship focus.

"But the fruit of the spirit is love, joy, peace,
patience, kindness, goodness,
faithfulness, gentleness, self-control..." (Galatians 5:22-23a)

APPROACH. Adjust It

When I asked God to show me what I needed to change in my life, the first piece of advice came to my mind in the form of the statement, ***"Act as if you are taken, and one day you will be."*** This hit me hard. This advice moved my mind off my needs and onto the development of genuine kindness and goodness.

I had grown accustomed to the normal, natural approach of watching females and evaluating. You may call it by a different name, or you may be completely naive to this approach. Every single person I have ever met, though, is entangled to some degree, and after we take a look at this approach you will have fun watching others perform it. Just sit back; observe the next time you are at a party, the gym, an airport, or any function where single men and women are in the same room. Most people assess the situation and evaluate his or her options. Could she be the one? I want to meet her! or How can I get his attention? And the list goes on. I was certainly pathetic at it, but diligent none the less. Then came the adjustment to my approach.

Act as if you are taken and one day you will be. I began to realize that 99.999% or more of all the women I came in contact with were someone else's wife. In God's eyes these women were already spoken for, if not already married.

I had several friends who were married and I began to notice how differently I treated their wives compared to the single women I would meet. The realization would come later that to develop genuine kindness and goodness, I must also adopt a new approach.

My biggest struggle was on a philosophical level. I tended to barter with God. "You see, God, if I act as if I'm in a relationship, then none of the women I come in contact with will be interested in me!" This would painfully reduce the already remote options available. In His still small voice, God replied by allowing me to realize that no one was interested in me anyway; so why not give it a try?

Try I did. The results were immediate and wonderful! No, I did not meet my wife the next day. I didn't even get a date for several more weeks. What I did get was FREEDOM. Most people never realize how much pressure we put on ourselves and how far off the "scope and evaluation" approach is.

The "new" approach made things so much easier. At the time I had no idea how this would reveal the woman of my dreams, but I experienced a freedom I had never known. Instead of entering functions with a mental evaluation chart, I began to approach every situation with no agenda, no expectations, and no pressure. I looked for opportunities to make others feel comfortable. I found it much easier to actually carry on a conversation when I did not feel the need to get something from it.

What I began experiencing was the character God wants to build into us and our relationships. This approach was simply the means to accomplish the task. God wants to make all of us desirable.

Now, who does not want to be desirable? God knows our hearts and has THE PLAN to make us desirable. Fortunately, it does not come from countless hours in a gym. Being desirable does not come from a big bank account, nor does it come from being the most popular person at a party. If you want to be desirable to the opposite sex, God has the answer in Proverbs, chapter 19. What would this information be worth to you?

To know the secret that all those of the opposite sex are looking for would be a relief. Do you want to be desirable? It is the character quality I found through the approach of acting like I was already taken; it is found in Proverbs 19:22.

"What is desirable in a man is his...KINDNESS."

How do we develop kindness? By adjusting our approach! Lose the agenda, drop the expectations, get freed up to learn how to be genuinely kind and good.

This was just the first of many qualities God wanted to produce in my life. I would later discover and begin to embody several attributes discussed in Galatians 5:22-23. Adjusting my approach, (acting "taken"), is the beginning to developing the kindness and goodness God knows are needed to make relationships work.

ATTITUDE. Refine It.

All is fair in love and war, right? Scanning the Bible cover to cover I have yet to find this verse. Few of us claim to have this as a core belief, yet it does exist in most of our attitudes in some form.

The second area of my life requiring reconstruction dealt with this need to refine my attitude. The statement that came to me illustrating how to deal with my attitude was: ***Date to develop faithfulness.*** We will go into great detail on the stages of dating in chapter 10, but for the purpose of our attitude discussion, allow me to simply define "going out" vs. "dating."

Going out is the act of having fun and encouraging someone with no implied or expressed commitment. Singles should go out as often as possible, and in as many different situations as possible before deciding to date any one person. For the purpose of discussion, dating will be defined as "two people mutually agreeing to encourage and build loyalty for the other's benefit." (Note the word mutually.)

We need to develop faithfulness with every one we come in contact with. Faithfulness is necessary for character building. Once again, God chose to use several situations in my life to establish and refine some of the character qualities mentioned in Gal. 5:22-23. The refinement of my attitude produced growth in the areas of faithfulness, gentleness, and peace. The areas grew in two different situations. The first was through faithfulness to a female friend.

Nancy and I had worked and taught together for several years at the same church. She was one of my best friends and gave great advice. Being a female, she saw things from a different perspective.

For those of you who have a close friend of the opposite sex, you will understand the outside pressure to define such a relationship. Most of this pressure comes from a well meaning family member or friends that do not understand.

After such pressure persisted for several years, we decided to see if dating was something we needed to do. After a couple weeks it was clear to me that this was not the "fit" everyone else had lobbied for. It just didn't click for me. Later I realized the feelings on her side were a bit stronger and we made a more committed effort. Awkward right?

My attitude was being shaped, and my loyalty to my friend was at stake. As painful as it was to be honest with my feelings that this wasn't a fit, ending it was the right thing to do. There is never an easy way to break off a dating relationship, but there is a godly way. Do it with a commitment to the other's well being. That may mean giving space. It may mean talking about hard issues and apologizing for being misleading. It may mean facing up to a wrong that was done. Whatever the action, the attitude must shift to a faithfulness for the other's good.

Pray for wisdom and sensitivity. She requested that I give space and time; to hold off going out with other women for a period of time so as to not dishonor her time of healing. I also made some mistakes, but God used them in the long run. I wanted to be so open to talk that I went overboard by calling too frequently. The reason I share all this is to communicate the need for a refined attitude. We must commit to getting our eyes off ourselves and onto faithfulness to those around us.

Another opportunity for faithfulness came with one of my roommates. No, I did not have any desire to date my roommate. The situation arose when we were both interested in a certain young lady. He expressed his interest in her to me just as I found out through a friend that she might be interested in me. How could I show faithfulness to my roommate Glenn and still go out with her? Enter God. Who is more important, a friend and roommate or a possible date?

Some of you would ask the deep theologically debated question, "What did she look like?" The thought more than crossed my mind. She was a beautiful girl and very sharp. For all I knew she did not even know Glenn existed. As I put it before the Lord, my role became painfully clear. How could I decrease and God increase in this situation? Developing faithfulness to Glenn was the only option.

A couple months passed. Glenn had been around her and had gone out with her a couple times. The spark never took. He had not talked much about her for some time, so he and I had a talk. We discussed his interest in her and how their times together had gone. His interest in her had worn off, according to Glenn, and there seemed to be no future with her other than a friendship. He inquired about why I wanted to know. When I told him I might want to ask her out he was all for it. I expressed to him that I did not want anything to come between our friendship, and if asking her out would cause any friction or even make him feel awkward, I wouldn't do it. His friendship was worth a lot more than a date.

If this sounded a bit too easy, let me assure you it was not. If refining our attitudes appears too difficult, you can bet it is. Our natural tendency is to be loyal to ourselves. The godly character needed to make and grow a wonderful relationship is not a natural one. It is only when we allow God to refine our attitude through faithfulness that we can experience the depth of such character qualities as gentleness and peace.

Through faithfulness to my friends and being sensitive for the first time to God's refinement of my attitude, I began to experience the development of gentleness. My personality can be very brash and overbearing. God allowed me to see that anyone and everyone can be gentle with a little refinement.

The greatest part of refinement in attitude may be the by-product. While faithfulness is a commitment and gentleness certainly takes time, the peace of God is such a sweet reward. As Paul describes in Philippians 4, His peace in relationships from faithfulness and gentleness are beyond comprehension. Allow God to refine your attitude about your relationships. Trust me, you do not want to miss the faithfulness, gentleness, and peace He has in store.

Actions. Mold Them.

Probably one of the most frequently pondered questions (with regard to dating relationships) is, "How far do we go physically before it is too far?" The answer to this question eluded me for most of my adult life. Some of the most thought provoking ideas I had ever heard were from Bible studies I attended. Dan DeHaan once said, "There is no right answer to a wrong question."

God desires us to be obedient to His Word. Tony Evans shared a great example by comparing sex to fire. When a fire is in a fireplace it provides great warmth and meets a vital need. When left unguarded and allowed out of the fireplace, it will destroy everything it touches. Marriage is the fireplace God designed for sex.[1]

Biblically speaking the issue is very clear. II Timothy 2:22 says, "Now flee from youthful lust..."[1] Exodus 20:14 "You shall not commit adultery." If those two verses don't clear up the issue, Hebrews 13:4 is crystal clear, "...marriage should be honored by all, and the marriage bed kept pure." Not much gray area there.

Your line may be way behind the biblical mark set forth by these verses, or right next to it, dangling one foot over the edge. I will not tell you where to draw the line, but I have to tell you the radical transformation God encouraged in my heart and how He molded my actions. You may feel as I did, that the answers never seemed practical and were most often overwhelmingly black and white with very little everyday application. Just don't do it!

Fortunately God is a personal God and does not stop there. He is willing to give wisdom to all who ask. I needed more wisdom, so I asked.

When we come to Him with a pure heart to know His best for us, we can ask any question and He will answer. After ruining several relationships by getting too involved too early, I decided to see what God would say. The lines I was drawing, although on the right side of scripture, were just not working. Committed to His Word and seeking to find some practical everyday answers, He impressed on my heart yet another statement that taught me even more about the character of Galatians 5:22-23. ***Keep special things special.***

What does that mean? This phrase was at the forefront of my mind for over a year after meeting my wife. I continued to return to the statement. This one phrase taught me what real love, lasting joy, true patience, and God empowering self-control were all about. I won't bore you with all the details of the time before we tied the knot, but I will share how God worked this principle into the reality of my relationships.

Heather and I had met, were dating, and things were great. She far exceeded all my dreams and was so wonderful in every situation we encountered. To be completely candid, I was ready to plant a kiss on her the second time we went out. Kenn's version of self-control was to wait at least one date before letting my hormones take over my lips. God's version was quite different.

Don't think for a minute the feeling just disappeared. I wanted more than anything to stake my claim and lock lips. Then came the inspired thoughts running through my mind, "Keep special things special." Several endings to dates left my insides in knots. Heather would later share her frustration as well.

"God, she is a babe and I really want to kiss her! It is within your limits, and I think she would kiss back!" If God ever chose to speak to me audibly it would have been then. He would probably have said something like, "Go ahead moron, mess this one up too!"

Instead, I pondered the Galatians passage and with much agony, prayed about the situation. "God, what do you mean, keep special things special?" I opened the Bible to Philippians and came across Chapter 2 verse 3.

Suddenly the question rang in my ear, "Why do you want to kiss her?"

"She is beautiful and cool and I really like her."

Then the first four words of that verse slapped me in the face, *"Do nothing from selfishness..."* Just because I wanted to was the worst reason of all.

After a few more dates, I could honestly say it was for her and not just for me. I knew she was more than open to the idea and I wanted her to feel special. The end of each evening we hugged, had several kind words, then a lean forward (face toward face), a quick turn, walk away and promise to call. God, why can I not get the green light here to kiss her?!!

During this time of waiting I was amazed at the creative ideas that were coming out of my two cell brain. I did not want this beautiful woman to walk away. Yet, I did not have the green light from God to do the obvious physical statement of affection, so I had to get creative. The down-side at the time, unknown to me, was what she was going through at work .

Each Monday Heather went into the teachers' lounge and the topic of her weekend would come up. "Seeing anybody?"

"Yeah, this guy named Kenn."

"Is he a good kisser?"

"I don't know; we haven't kissed yet."

Jaws dropped and she would get the strangest looks. Each week the looks got stranger. Heather worked with some nice people, but they had no concept of what the Christian life is like, so the idea of dating someone for a month and not sleeping together (much less kissing) was a big shock.

My shock came when the "okay" seemed on the horizon. The timing was right, but there was one more verification question. "Kenn, would you kiss her in front of her father?" That one took me a couple more days, but I came to grips with a firm "Yes," and was ready to go. I was out the door ready to pucker up. Then that phrase hit me again. "Keep special things special." My heart's molded into the right shape. I'd tell her dad if the situation arose. What now?

"Make it special... honor her... kiss her so she would never forget it." Cool idea. The creative steam of thoughts went into overdrive. It is amazing what we can do when we are motivated. I had never even considered this idea of keeping it special, much less to the extent that God and I got real personal. Ideas flew through my head and the perfect idea began to fall into place.

The place was really the only thing special about it. I was just going full time as a speaker and comedian, so money was tight if there was any at all. Time was also a rare commodity and an open weekend was nearly nonexistent. All the pieces fell into place, however, and we were headed out for the evening. Our big evening was eating dinner at a fast food place and taking in a dollar movie.

We finished the fine dining experience and the timing was perfect. I told her I had some place I wanted to show her before the movie, and off we went. I know God was giving me a bit of encouragement when we pulled up to the square of the town where we live. The song I wanted to play for her, but did not have, came on the radio. I was blown away.

Heather pointed out the song and sighed at how much this song reminded her of us. "Where are we going?" she wondered out loud. I told her she would soon see as we parked at the square. "What is here," she asked. I took her hand and we walked through the square up to one of the cutest gazebos you'll ever find.

I turned to face her and held her ever so gently. "Heather, I have wanted to do this since the first time I saw you, but I wanted it to be special. Something to show you how special you are." Then I leaned over and softly kissed her as she melted. (I have never had a woman melt in my arms before.) Trust me, you want this experience. I am not trying to express any false humility or coax a pat on the back, but quite honestly, I am not smart enough to think of something so great. Never would I think of being patient enough to pull off something like this on my own.

Had it not been for God's guidance I never would have shown the self-control needed, practice the patience required, or experienced the rush of joy and the depth of love that I had only imagined. The bottom line is that God is willing and able to teach us the character qualities needed. He knows about love and joy beyond our dreams, but it is up to us to trust Him. It is up to us to allow Him to mold our actions.

These actions made an incredible impact on our relationship with one another. The next Monday at school the other teachers once again began to examine Heather's poor dating life. "Did he kiss you yet?..." She smiled, paused, and told them the entire story. Someone walked by the lounge during the climax of the story, and seeing women crying, stopped to ask what was wrong.

The teachers knew Heather was a Christian and had often chastised her for thinking she could find someone with the character she often described. I am so thankful that for once I chose to allow God to mold that character into my actions.

Allowing God to adjust our approach is not natural for most of us. Opening up to have Him refine our attitude is not natural. Committing to trust God as we allow Him to mold our actions is not natural. But, for those who make these hard choices, it is very much worth it.

In retrospect, it is easy to see the results produced by all the character qualities from Galatians 5:22-23. These character qualities must be established and strengthened in our personal lives and in our relationships to discover God's best for our lives.

[1] Evans, Tony. *The Urban Alternative* Radio Program. March, 1996.
[2] NAS

BECOMING Love

CHAPTER EIGHT

Becoming A Great Lover

*Equations To Becoming
A Great Lover*

*G*od wants you to be a great lover. The Bible (yes, the Bible) makes it known to us, and we are going to take a very close look at two equations in fulfilling this glorious task. The difficulty in these equations is not in the understanding of the factors (or qualities) involved, but in the discipline in carrying them out. Use a cheat sheet if you would like, but do not misunderstand the clear factors involved in the equations of becoming a great lover.

THE FIRST EQUATION

Having traveled over most of the country, it has become evident to me that a large majority of singles are very much alike in their quest for someone of the opposite sex. The order of the qualities may differ between men and women, but the categories are pretty much the same. In my unofficial survey of well over two thousand singles from all over, of all ages, and of both sexes, I have found some interesting insights. (It is important to note, however, this part of the first equation is going to vary for everyone.) Honesty with yourself is the most critical factor of this equation.

Below is a list of the top things men and women look for in a member of the opposite sex. Does this sound like some vital information? It is crucial to evaluate the information found in the first equation in two ways.

The two major categories of evaluation are CAN DO and JUST YOU. There are certain aspects of who we are that we do have some control over; these go into the CAN DO category. Some actual examples from real people surveyed are: a non-smoker, punctuality, shoe style, healthy teeth, and fragrance. (I'm not clear on what they meant by fragrance so we will move on).

The other category lists areas we have no control over or JUST YOU. This would be things like age, red hair, height and eyes (I guess they were looking for someone with eyes). As you look over these qualities, please do not stress out if you see something that is a JUST YOU quality and worry that you are just five feet tall and they're looking for a runway model.

I mentioned that honesty is important in this equation and those who took part in the survey were honest as well. Although these are not in any particular order, this first factor was a popular one.

One of the common factors in both the men and women's lists is **Physical appearance**. Let's clear up a couple of misconceptions right away. First of all, it is normal to notice someone's physical appearance. James Dobson put it very well on his radio program when he said, "If anyone ever tells you his or her first encounter was something other than eye to body contact, they are either talking on a phone or lying."

The first thing we notice is a person's physique. Biblically, we can look at Genesis 29:11. It does not say, "Jacob saw Rachel and she appeared to have a great personality." Jacob noticed her face and her form. We do not know what her face and form looked like, but we do know Jacob must have thought it was worth his attention and seven years worth of work.

Many people have a theological hang up thinking it is not appropriate to be attracted to another. What they don't realize is that God made us that way! Often, those who have an aversion to admitting looks are important are people with poor self esteem. The main reason I know this is because I lived through that phase for years. Who is to say what is beautiful and what is ugly? Beauty is certainly in the eye of the beholder.

My personal advice is to marry someone you believe is the most beautiful complete package in the world. I did. If I am going to be with someone for the rest of my life, I don't want to settle for anything but the best. Being a reformed poor self-image guy, I am amazed to this day that God created someone who is as gorgeous as my wife who thinks I am attractive too. When we put our total trust in our loving heavenly Father, He will bless us beyond our dreams. Physical appearance may be at the top of your list or not at all. Looks are certainly part of the package, but remember this is your list, and you can put anything in it you feel is important to your total package. What factors are you looking for?

Another popular quality is **Sense of Humor**. I could not agree more with this choice. Having been married now for a while, I see first hand the importance of being able to laugh together on a regular basis.

Let's face facts. There are going to be a lot of trivial things that will either drive you crazy or provide a good laugh. One that instantly comes to mind is when dealing with hair. It amazes me how much women can lose and still have any left on their head.

Heather, my wife, teaches school so she takes the first shower each morning. The opportunity for a great laugh comes when I take mine. I look in the drain and there is all this mangled hair at my feet. There is a small toupee in the drain. Now I could allow this to get to me all the time, or simply laugh it off. Of course I have chosen to laugh it off!

Singles will often ask how one knows if this person or that person is the right one. My response is to tell them I don't know. I can however give you a great acid test to reveal if it is the wrong person or wrong time. If you decide to date and go out three or four times without having a good gut laugh, it is most likely not right. It is very important for someone to be able to laugh at themselves. A good sense of humor also indicates a genuine openness. Look for that ability to laugh; it is priceless.

Many people, both men and women, put great value on the **Honesty/Openness** factor. A phrase that came up describing this quality was, what you see is what you get. After talking with scores of singles, it became obvious to me that a little hurt now, while being honest, beats a lot of hurt down the road. Honesty and openness are such necessary qualities to develop. They are vital for any relationship to grow.

You might ask, "What if I'm not in a relationship?" That question I posed to God when the thought first crossed my mind. Honesty and openness can and will start when we look in the mirror. Ask if you are being honest with yourself, and if you are truly happy with yourself. Accepting how God has created us and being thankful for who we are is a huge first step. When praying, ask God for insight if you have a hard time identifying your own biggest hurdle. Two great questions to ask are, "If I could change one thing about myself what would it be, and why?"

One of the biggest initial hurdles for me was accepting the physical package I had been given. After years of struggle, I honestly looked in the mirror and thought about the face and package God had created. My first thought was, "Well I am kind of cute in a Benji , mutt dog sort of way." Your struggle may not be physical appearance. It may be your job, your past, your circumstances, etc. It is important that we come to the point where we can honestly and openly say, "What you see is what you get." Believe it or not, people really do long to find honesty and openness in someone.

Another factor both men and women ranked very highly was **Character**. Words like loyal, responsible, trustworthy, faithful, and kind were used to describe the ideal person. Since we have already gone into great detail on this topic we need only to review chapter six and mark the specific qualities we desire most. A wonderful resource on character is the book of Ruth. Ladies especially can glean from this timeless example of becoming a woman of excellence. In short, Ruth was a foreigner with no family status who came from the bottom of the social ladder, yet the most handsome successful man pursued and married her because of her character.[1]

While character is a CAN DO, another factor equally important is in the JUST YOU category... **Personality**. Take a look at some of the qualities mentioned in response to my survey: outgoing, shy, even tempered, laid back, optimistic, down to earth. Now if you can accomplish all of these, you need serious personality disorder help – not a relationship! A good way to view personality is to be yourself. Know your strengths and weaknesses. It is very important to find the balance between being completely ourselves, happy with who we are, and yet never excusing poor behavior by telling others, "That's just the way I am, take it or leave it!" We need to allow our personalities to explain who we are, but never used as an excuse for our behavior.

The final factor is actually the most popular and highest in priority on a vast majority of surveys. Most quality singles are looking for a **Christian**. Not by name only, but by lifestyle. Here are just a few of the phrases used to describe the type Christian desired: sold out, growing, close in a walk with God, spiritual leader, loves God more than anything including me. Interesting? The main thrust of this factor was the personal and growing nature with God involved. Not just a go-to-church be-a-good-person type, but someone who really understands what a relationship with the Lord was all about.

I am very impressed with all of those who stated these qualities. The real test, though, is what happens next. Remember this is an equation. Now it's your turn. List the top five most important factors you look for in someone of the opposite sex. Again, this only works if you are completely honest. Also, you may have other factors that are not listed previously. That's great. Be as unique and detailed as possible. You cannot be too specific. Do not read any further until you have made your list.

1) Completely & totally in love with God.

2) Servant

3) Loving/Compassionate

4) Patient

5) Enjoys life.

Now the moment of truth. Have you filled in your top five? When you have with the utmost honesty and clarity, you are ready for the rest of the first equation.

Believe it or not, this equation will not take superior math skills to complete. However, two math terms describe this next step perfectly. It is time to reverse the focus and multiply the qualities. The first time the Lord brought this exercise to my mind I became excited about the thought of God creating my perfect list into a wife. What I soon realized was this equation was not for anyone else but me.

After compiling the list of high standards and dream factors, the Lord impressed on my heart to reverse and multiply. Take the list and make it a mirror, not a microscope. The discovery was that this list was not for the evaluation of potential dates, rather it was the standard for me to become. **Become your list!** Not just in word or category, but multiply the qualities to the point of perfection. Our efforts must shift from outward evaluation to inward application.

What factors are on your list? Are you a perfect representation of those factors? What plan can you devise to become those factors?

THE SECOND EQUATION

The second equation includes the factors needed for you to become your list. Just as addition and subtraction are basic and fundamental for any equation to work, so will our second set of factors equal a fool-proof, never fail plan to become what we look and long for most. What are these basic factors and how does this second equation work? The answer is found in I Corinthians 13:4-8a.

When most Christians hear that scripture reference they think 'The Love Chapter.' You are correct. When God first laid this equation on my heart I thought the same thing and began to intellectually tune out. Then the Lord rocked me with an uncomfortable set of thoughts. Before I could open to the passage I had to answer some very painful questions.

Love is something many of us strongly desire, but too often we do not even know the real definition. I am embarrassed to think I desired love in my life, but did not even know completely what love was. It can be painfully evident that too often we know where to find a certain truth, we know about it, and have even taken part of it to heart, but fail to finish the definition. Partial credit on a math test may be acceptable, but in life and love we must finish the whole equation to experience the correct answer.

We will take a brief look at all fifteen factors defining God's definition of Love, but before we do, can you name all the factors? Without looking, list as many factors of love you think are in the passage we are about to learn:

Now look up I Corinthians 13:4-7 in your Bible or simply look below. How did you do?

This passage provides such a versatile definition. It was written to the church at Corinth with regard to the love God desires all believers to have within any church body. These components of love can be applied in a huge variety of situations. See if you can find a need for application in one of these I WISH situations.

I WISH I had a loving relationship that met the desire I have within me.

I WISH I knew if this was "the one" for me. Can someone really know?

I WISH my spouse understood and loved me more.

This passage and these factors fulfill every one of those wishes, but in a very different way than one might think.

The natural view of love is to enjoy what we get out of it. God's factors are first and foremost what we give, not get, out of love. The answer to fulfilling our wish is not determined by the uncontrollable whims of someone else. The magic of this wish lies within us. Do we have the desire and discipline to know and practice these factors of love and thus become the very person God desires us to be? Is it not interesting that so many of us want a growing, lasting, fulfilling love, but do not even know what it is? The world's greatest lover will not only know, but will embody these factors as well. Let's take a brief look at them.

Patience or long suffering. This is an infinite capacity to endure.

Kindness or mercy. Now the patience thing is okay, but this word 'kindness' is just a bit too difficult to swallow. Kind does not simply mean to be nice whenever possible. This word in its original context means something far more. Picture if you will someone giving you a gift you really wanted. Now picture how you would feel knowing you had already bought the gift they wanted and needed most in the whole world and joyfully lavished it upon them in reciprocation. The kindness mentioned here is that joyous response but to the opposite prompt.

What Paul is saying here is when someone treats you badly, you treat them with a joyous, need -meeting response. I don't know about you, but that is just not natural. Oh, sure I can be mistreated by other people and not complain, but push the wrong buttons too many times and you would have wished you hadn't. This factor is challenging us to resist reaction and respond to ill treatment with joyous care.

Then Paul goes into a list of selfish factors that really hit the very nature of most of our actions. *Love is not jealous.* There is no competition in love. So much for the "all is fair in love and war" philosophy. Love looks out for someone's good without regard for self. Even the conversation focuses on others. *Love does not brag and is not arrogant.* True love is more interested in giving praise and attention than gaining anything. Then there is the action factor. *Love is not unbecoming* and *does not seek its own favor.* Love seeks first, foremost, and always the good of others in approach and actions. By putting others in the spotlight, love acts honorably to shed light on those around. Love's purpose is always the edification and illumination of others.

Paul not only shares how to give the proper actions, he also illustrates how not to take the improper actions. *Love is not provoked* and *does not take into account a wrong suffered.* Instantly several relationships come to mind where I have been wronged. This quality of love accounts only the good and relinquishes all debts. Along with the forgiving all debts comes the mind set of never allowing new debts to occur. Love is never touchy and doesn't allow anything to lessen its focus on giving wholeheartedly.

Love's wholehearted factor is also not influenced by outside sources. *Love does not rejoice in unrighteousness, but rejoices in the truth.* Our society has become overwhelmed by violence and suffering. The newsrooms of today live for any immoral or evil headline. Christ lived in a time of turmoil yet walked, lived, and breathed peace. Rejoicing in the truth is to ask the questions, "What would Jesus do, say, think?"

Then there are my favorite factors of all. *Bears all things, Believes all things, Hopes all things, Endures all things.* The word 'bears' denotes a conscience choice to cover. Love is not blind; it knows what is really there, but chooses to cover it up permanently. Love doesn't stop with simply forgiving the past. Believes all things says, "Your slate is clean with me and you are free."

Junior high was not a time of liberty for me. It seems teachers from year to year pass on the names of who they think are the problem students. My name topped that list in seventh grade. The first week of school I was put in the hot seat in every class except one. Mrs. Cherry's science class was my haven and my chance to start all over. She lived out the quality of believing the good in everyone. I remember the first day of her class. She announced, "All of you have a clean slate with me. As far as I am concerned you are all wonderful until you prove me otherwise."

I would have died before proving her wrong. She gave me a chance to live up to her expectations, not my past. After a few months, I got kind of comfortable in my new found graces. A homework assignment was too long and bothersome, so my best friend and I decided to do only half each and copy the other's work. We thought we were so smart until we were asked to stay behind after class the day after we turned in the homework.

Mrs. Cherry lived the true meaning of love once again. She didn't cut us any slack, rather she called us on it and gave us both zeros. My greatest fear was being realized. I had failed again and had proven her wrong. I was a no good cheat, and she had proof.

Then love hoped all things. Not in a gullible optimistic way, but in a tough and tender balance. She said the words that broke my heart and healed it all at once, "I am so disappointed in you. I never thought you of all people would do something like this." My heart was broken. She went on, "I know this is not you. I will give you a zero this time, but you are never going to do this again. You know better and this just is not the way you are." My heart healed with a second chance. Leon Morris puts it beautifully, "Hoping all things means to never take failure as final."[2]

The final factor is the effort of love. Endures all things does not mean a resigned patience, but an active, consistent, steady plodding forward. The picture painted here is one of a military leader going into battle. Amidst the worst of circumstances, he remains completely focused on advancing. With explosions all around and fear about to burst within, he presses forward. Love certainly endures. It is with this quality we have a choice to make. Will we endure? The truth is clear. The equation is set. The qualities are faultless. We are committed to know, do, and become love.

The steps in this equation are very simple, but hard to embody. First, understand this is a definition of how completely God loves us.

He chooses to cover our faults; He believes not what we are, but what He has made us to become. He refuses to take failure as final, and He endures to the bitter end regardless of the circumstances. His is the love that does not fail. God longs for you and I to become that same love. Choosing to understand His love is the first step, comprehension.

The second step is application. James 1:22-25 challenges us perfectly. Are we going to be an effectual doer or a forgetful hearer? Will we be the type that accepts and believes the truth and with a complete understanding places these qualities into our lives?

One of the most practical applications I have seen is to take one quality per day and simply do it. There is a group of teachers who heard this point and took it to heart. They shared with me their method of taking one quality per day and holding each other accountable to applying it. This process goes on for thirty days (each factor twice). What a great way to put it into practice! The equation is simple: Truth + Application + Honest Evaluation + Reconciliation back to the Truth = Love that Never Fails.

If we genuinely desire relationships that will never fail, we must learn these equations and become these qualities. God desires us to be the world's greatest lovers. The challenge is set, and the truth is clear. Will you do it?

[1] The book of Ruth.

[2] Morris, Leon. *Tyndale New Testament Commentaries*; (Grand Rapids, MI: W.M.B. EERDMANS PUB. Co. 1961) p.186.

CHAPTER NINE

Attitude Of Gratitude

Secrets of Love
Expect Nothing & Appreciate Everything

*L*ittle Chad was a shy, quiet young man. One day he came home and told his mother that he'd like to make a valentine for everyone in his class. Her heart sank. She thought, "I wish he wouldn't do that!" She had watched the children when they walked home from school. Her Chad was always behind them. They laughed and hung on to each other and talked to each other, but Chad was never included. Nevertheless, she decided she would go along with her son. So she purchased the paper and glue and crayons. For three weeks, night after night, Chad painstakingly made 35 valentines.

Valentine's Day dawned, and Chad was beside himself with excitement. He carefully stacked them up, put them in a bag, and bolted out the door. His mother decided to bake him his favorite cookies and serve them nice and warm with a cool glass of milk when he came home from school. She just knew he would be disappointed and maybe that would ease the pain a little. It hurt her to think that he wouldn't get many valentines-maybe none at all.

That afternoon she had the cookies and milk on the table. When she heard the children outside, she looked out the window. Sure enough, there they came, laughing and having the best time. And, as always, there was Chad in the rear. He walked a little faster than usual. She fully expected him to burst into tears as soon as he got inside. His arms were empty, she noticed, and when the door opened she choked back the tears.

"Mommy has some cookies and milk for you," she said.

But he hardly heard her words. He just marched right on by, his face aglow, and all he could say was: "Not a one. Not a one."

Her heart sank.

And then he added, "I didn't forget a one, not a single one!"[1]

Proper attitude when approaching love is vital. To be in love we must first become love ourselves (as defined in Chapter 8). One important way to accomplish this is with one of the most important attitude correcting statements in all of scripture located in Philippians 2:3 *"Do nothing from selfishness or empty conceit..."*

We will be hard pressed to find anyone who genuinely wants a love relationship and boldly proclaims him or herself conceited or selfish. The difficult part is when we honestly evaluate our lives and allow God to reveal the areas that are selfish and empty. Even more difficult is the process of allowing the needed changes to take place. When God began to work on the selfishness and conceit in my life, I clearly saw the depth of the problem.

I considered myself the last person on the earth who could be deemed selfish, but I later discovered selfishness had been cleverly covered by good intentions. Several relationships had ended and I cried out to the Lord for answers. "Lord why didn't this one work out? I gave my whole heart and was still hurt again!"

After the pity party, Philippians 2:3 came across my devotion time. Praying for meaning for my life, I discovered my attitude of self-ishness. I was giving wholeheartedly, ten-fold, hoping and expecting only to get a little something in return. That was the mistake; I was giving to get. Even expecting a small return, giving to get is selfish and does not accomplish God's will. It is a wrong attitude.

Another wrong attitude that seems so natural is that of conceit. None of us wants to be thought of as conceited. You will not want to begin a conversation on a first date with, "My best quality is my conceit." The heart of conceit is when we stop improving on the areas we know need work, and instead evaluate others by our list. We judge ourselves by our ideals and others by their actions. It is so innocent, yet so natural to focus outwardly.

Several roommates and friends used to talk about the invisible checklist that accompanied each date. We would joke about things like, "After you opened her door did she reach over and unlock yours?" (ten points.) "Did she say thank you at the right time?" The list went on and on. If we are honest, we all have a list. This is another wrong attitude.

We will not embody godly qualities by evaluating others. Always remember that God works from the inside out. Our happiness does not hinge on how picky we can be with someone else. The successes of our relationships are determined by how well we embody the qualities and attitudes of love. Well, you may ask, if selfishness and empty conceit are the wrong attitudes, what are the correct attitudes? This is a great question answered in Philippians 2:3-4.

EXPECT NOTHING

"But with humility of mind..."[2] (Philippians 2:3) What is humility of mind? It is not a degrading of ourselves. Humility is not saying, we are nothing, worse than a worm, no, worse than a worm in a well, no worse than a worm in a dry well in the cracks of the dirt, no ... you get the picture. Humility is having a proper perspective with regard to our Heavenly Father. Many singles and unhappy married people today lack the proper perspective of humility. We ask God, "Why don't you give me the relationship I desire? Why am I not in a relationship that will make me happy?"

After a long look at this, I realized my understanding of and attitude towards humility were all wrong. God has already done it all. Why am I asking the God, who controls it all, why He is not changing to meet my needs? My attitude must change to ask in humility of mind, "God how do you want me to change in order to experience what you have already planned?"

We must come to realize God owes us nothing! He has lived the perfect example of love for us, taken all our faults and failure, and died for them so we could be free. Upon request He lives within us to guide and direct us when we are willing to listen. He owes us nothing. He has given us everything, and in our foolishness we ask for something He has already provided.

If we desire love in our lives, we must seek Him with all of our hearts and seek to become all He is. We must shift to a non-expectant attitude that humbly says, "God if You never did another thing for me, You have done enough." At that point we will begin to have the scales fall from our eyes and see the love He has already provided.

I heard from a well-meaning Christian wife who believed she married the wrong man and felt she would never be happy. What a sad attitude! Not to over simplify things, but the problem in this woman's life is most likely not the wrong man, but her wrong attitude. She is obviously expecting this man to be something or do something which she has decided he is incapable of accomplishing. She lacks a key attitude. Expecting Nothing. This includes dying to self. Look at the progression Jesus took in Philippians 2:5-9.

Humble, Servant, Obedient
Death, Cross, God Exalted

If we are going to have a successful marriage and have edifying relationships, we must learn the attitude of dying to one's self. This phrase appears often in the Christian walk, and only recently have I understood its meaning. I thought dying to self meant a complete apathy toward an area of life. If people didn't care about relationships, how could they getting married? Does it mean to avoid someone of the opposite sex and have God reveal us to one another in a dream, and then show up at the alter having never seen our mate? To some singles that may not sound too bad.

God's plan is much better and more reasonable. Dying to self is an active pursuit of our Heavenly Father's way. Simply put, it is to **do it God's way or no way at all**. When we choose this route, we relinquish control. We trust in God to make things happen. Remember clearly in Jesus' life how he was wronged, His rights violated, His life taken, but for trust in God the Father, His created purpose was fulfilled.

If you are single and have a desire to be in a relationship, then you must realize God has given you that desire, and it is part of His purpose for your life. Now, to realize that desire within His perfect plan, we must die to self. Our attitude must be the one of doing it God's way or no way at all. Our expectations must turn completely inward and our lives must begin to align with His word, His will, and His way. Our expectation of others must become zero, and must focus inward to how we are becoming who God desires us to be.

Expecting Nothing is an attitude adjustment toward God and toward ourselves, but most practically toward others. We must set our attitude toward others as having no agenda and no evaluation, thus no expectations. Love is first and foremost what we give. Jesus states the attitude we must have in Luke 6:35.

*"But love your enemies, and do good, and lend, **expecting nothing** in return; and your reward will be great, and you will be sons of the Most High; for He Himself is kind to ungrateful and evil men."* [3]

I know God has a sense of humor. He chose to teach me this verse in a very practical way through dating. I started learning the truths shared in this book and thought I was ready to apply them to my life. God had His agenda to teach me the attitude of expecting nothing. Often we hear that we don't appreciate something until it is gone. We cannot appreciate the good until we experience the bad. The bad happened to me.

After meeting a quite attractive woman at a social gathering, we talked intermittently throughout the evening and really seemed to hit it off. This conversation lead to her phone number, and I soon asked her to dinner. After going dateless for several months, I thought this was God's reward.

Have you ever met someone and based on one conversation built them up in your mind to be the perfect person? She was Miss America, Mother Theresa, and Julia Roberts all wrapped up into one package. This was going to be worth the long wait and countless efforts! We talked and set the dinner date. I felt this was certainly going to be a night to remember. And it certainly was! From the time I picked her up until the time we parted ways it was a disaster.

She had something negative to say about everything! If it could be critiqued, it was. The way I spoke on the phone, the restaurant, the evenings plans, what I was wearing, even the route I took taking her home were all criticized and butchered. When it was finally over, I sank into my car with a huge sigh of relief and could not help but ask God on my long drive home, "What was that for?"

Sorting through the evening, I began to realize this horrible experience's purpose. Expect nothing. When we expect nothing it is impossible to be let down. From that night forward no woman's actions could have possibly been worse. God in His grace and humor taught me to expect nothing of others.

We must learn to expect nothing from God; He has already given us everything we need. Expecting nothing means to die to ourselves that God might exalt us. We must expect nothing from others so that we will never be disappointed.

Jesus commands us to expect nothing when He spoke of loving and giving to our enemies. It is imperative that this attitude be fundamental in the relationships with those we do want to be with. The first absolute attitude is to...***Expect Nothing!***

APPRECIATE EVERYTHING

Everyone likes to be appreciated. Genuine appreciation comes in many forms and is always welcome. Every time I open the mail box I look through the bills and junk mail hoping to find anything that is hand written. It has such a personal touch. We feel so appreciated when someone takes the time to simply write us or say hello. What a great action to signify appreciation.

Paul writes in Philippians 2:3 another absolute attitude, "each of you regard one another as more important than himself."[4] If we want to move forward in our quest for happy and successful relationships, we must develop an attitude of gratitude.

In some areas it is easy after thirty years of being single, and after a difficult but very worthwhile process of change, I got married. I had been conditioned while single that if it was going to get done around the house I was going to have to be the one to do it.

The first few months of marriage were unbelievable. I would come home thinking of a hundred things to get done before my next trip only to find my wife had done half of them already and even started many others. The laundry was already in the dryer, the house was dusted, bills paid, calls returned. WOW! Thank you, Thank you, Thank you! We both realized the benefit of an expect nothing attitude by doing for one another. The appreciation just followed.

A problem occurs when what once was appreciated is now expected. We must fight with all our heart, soul and mind to never fall into the trap of forgetting how to appreciate the other person in our relationship. We must continuously set our mind and hearts on being appreciative of the basics.

Heather and I recently enjoyed a great attitude of gratitude re-set. Metro Bible Study in Atlanta has a group that has been going down town each Friday night for the past twenty years. This group is not going to the theater, a ball game, or a concert. They go to the same empty parking lot each week to meet with the homeless.

A couple of the people put the event together by rounding up food and some donated clothes. There is music, a message, and then dinner and clothes to be passed out. Mostly it is a time to give and encourage. This experience ranks as one of the richest I have personally ever been involved with. Jesus said, *"...whatever you did for one of the least of these brothers of mine you did for me."* [5] I saw Jesus up close and personal through the eyes of these homeless people.

Jesus also said, *"The poor you will always have with you..."* [6] I do not know what city you live in, but I do know there are needs in your community. This type of ministry is not for everyone, but it is a great way to focus on this principle of expecting nothing and appreciating everything. Finding a group that is involved with meeting needs is relatively easy. Making the time to invest in others lives is never wasted time. These types of projects establish a lasting memory of what it means to expect nothing and appreciate everything.

Appreciation can also erode when we begin taking others for granted. When was the last time we took the five minutes to write a note to someone who encourages us? When was the last time we did something we were not required to for someone who really needed encouragement? Are we looking for opportunities to show appreciation or simply waiting to notice when everybody else does? Genuine appreciation takes place by choice not by reaction.

This was never more evident than when I heard an elderly couple respond to a question about marriage. Some friends were making a video for a couple who were soon to be married. Not only did they capture the comments and advice from numerous friends and family, they went one better. Toting a video camera, they went to our city square and asked total strangers to give a good luck message.

Many offered best wishes or offered advice.

The videographer later came across an elderly couple holding hands walking in the square. They approached and asked if they would be willing to take part in this endeavor. The couple agreed, and the camera rolled. The sweet couple was asked how long they had been married and if they had any advice for the couple to be. "Fifty-one years," replied the wife with a shy smile.

And what advice did they have for the soon-to-be couple? The gentleman paused, squeezed his wife's hand and said, "Oh, I don't know much about advice. I guess you just don't take each other for granted. Every week for the last fifty-one years we have had a date. It's what we are doing right now. I guess that would be it."

What an answer! Each week for the past half a century he asks his bride for a night out. For half a century she has said yes. Isn't that precious? Appreciation takes time. Appreciation takes effort.

Watching as the couple walked away holding hands smiling, it sure seemed worth it. I am certain over those fifty-one years they had learned the importance of appreciating everything. One of the key attitudes of appreciating everything is to not take anything for granted.

Appreciating the basics is important. Not taking things for granted is vital, but let's take a quantum leap and look at another key to appreciating everything. The writer of Hebrews states it very well in verse 10:24, "let us consider how to stimulate one another to love and good deeds."[7] One of the greatest ways to appreciate is to stimulate. There, it even rhymes.

Take the time and think about who or what encourages you during a week. Then invest the time and effort to let whomever is responsible know about it. Too often we neglect others, feeling sure he already knows or she must have many people encouraging her. The more I talk with people, the more I realize there is a huge deficit of genuine appreciation. The next time you think you don't need to show appreciation ask yourself when the last time was that someone took the time and effort to appreciate you?

As I continue to learn this attitude of gratitude, the opportunities seem to be everywhere; I just have to take the time to look. My wife and I were on our way to church and turned on the radio. We found a station playing some really upbeat non-liturgical Christian music. A lot of the best tunes with some great beat. Heather wondered what station was playing. We looked down to see that it was one of the major secular stations in our city. They had set aside some time on Sunday morning to play the most upbeat Christian stuff they could find. It may not be for everyone, but we sure liked it.

We talked about taping the show so we could enjoy it during the week. Heather said, "We need to write them a tell them this is great." My first thought was that they already knew, but she was right. Here was a station taking a chance, and it really encouraged us. I began to think of the other areas of life I had been encouraged and almost immediately someone came to mind. James Cook.

James is a custodian at a local Junior High school. He is also one of the most faithful prayer warriors I know. Each week at the Metro Bible Study he volunteers to take all the prayer requests and prays over each one. After they are shared with the group they are handed over to James. Of the hundreds of people attending, there may be a handful that know about James.

God prompted my heart with, "You know about him; do something." It was a simple note that took maybe five minutes to write. It is important that he knew someone appreciated his faithful efforts and that he was encouraged to continue what he was doing. Who is the James in your life? We see them every day. Whose day can you make a little brighter? It doesn't take being in a relationship to develop this attitude.

If you happen to be in a relationship here is another idea. (If you are not, then ear mark this page and come back to it.) A big key to appreciation is initiation. Appreciation is most often communicated by simple effort. Take what is common, add some effort, and what do you get? Something special. Some friends of mine in the past were masters at this.

One time they had the idea of going to dinner and a movie. Pretty common right? Here is the kicker. These guys invited me to get involved in the planning. We decided on a group date so no one would feel out of place (And so I wouldn't have to go dateless). There was a movie coming out that everyone wanted to see. We added some extra effort and abracadabra...special.

The men went to the fast food restaurant selling the commemorative plastic cups for the movie we wanted to see. After collecting several cups, we planned a picnic for the evening at a local park. The guys gave the ladies an invitation that said when to meet us and where (map included). Upon their arrival we enjoyed a picnic dinner together and the question eventually came up, "What movie are we going to see?"

We answered, "Look at your cups!" They wanted to see that movie, but knew it was sold out that particular weekend. (But not if you had a friend stand in line at 4:00pm for tickets.) They were so surprised at how we got the tickets. This may sound corny, but you would not believe the mileage we got from that evening.

We would have seen the movie anyway, but we decided to take a little time and add some effort for it to become a night to remember. It was funny to be at parties after months had passed and one of those cups would show up. Without fail the story was told by an appreciative participant. All the ladies were very impressed with our creativity.

Appreciation takes time. Appreciation takes effort. But, to see a face light up, and a heart filled with joy make it certainly worth the effort. How does God desire to develop an attitude of gratitude in you? Are we thanking God for the basics of life afforded us today? Who are the people in our influence that could benefit from a word of appreciation? Are we taking anyone for granted? Have we considered how to stimulate someone to love and to do good deeds today? Take something common in your day today; add some effort and see how special God can make you in someone's life.

Write down in the space below three people you appreciate. Now write down three to five ways to show appreciation. Match an expression of appreciation with each person. Try not to do the same for each in order to practice variety. Write down the date of a realistic deadline, and go for it.

Draw a box next to each person's name and when the effort is put forth, put a check in the box. This exercise may be easier or more difficult than you think. The important part is to do it. Through your efforts God will begin to mold in you an attitude of gratitude not to mention make someone's day very special.

[1]Galloway, Dale. *A 3rd Serving of Chicken Soup For The Soul.*
(Deerfield Beach, FL. Health Communications, Inc. 1996)
[2]NAS
[3]NAS (Emphasis added)
[4]NAS
[5]Matt. 25:40
[6]Matt. 26:11
[7]NAS

CHAPTER TEN

Plan And Promise

Relationships –
Time, Effort and Reward

*W*hat kind of marriage do you want? I know some singles reading this might say, "Hey, I just want a date." Dates lead eventually to marriages, so lets take a look. How about a marriage of love, joy, and peace? A spouse who is patient, kind, and gentle. What about a relationship marked by faithfulness, godliness, and self-control? It sounds pretty good doesn't it? If you offered this to people, most would accept. So why are most marriages and relationships not marked by these qualities? The answer is the same as the answer to my sixteenth birthday. (It is a stretch, but hang with me.)

A sixteen year old wants to drive as badly as a single person wants a relationship. A few days before my 16th birthday my father asked me if I would like a car when I turned sixteen. His question was met with an obvious, "Yeah!" Much to my shock He asked the exciting question, "What kind would you like?"

My mind began to race. I would spare him the Ferrari and go for the more practical 300ZX. After sharing my dream he asked what color, and why the 300ZX? The explanation was well received and everything was going great until my bubble burst. My father responded, "That sounds great! How are you going to be able to afford such a nice car?"

My dream ended more abruptly than it had begun. I told him I couldn't afford it. My father then explained a lesson of life I am still learning. "You can afford one, but it will cost you. You will have to work hard and save every penny. In a few years you could buy the car." I had to decide if new car was worth the effort, time, and sacrifice.

A relationship marked by love, joy, peace, patience, kindness, goodness, faithfulness, and self- control is far more valuable than any car will ever be. The tragic lesson to learn is that many people do not want to put in the time and effort to make it happen. This chapter is about the plan and the promise to those who choose to desire God's best. Galatians 6:7 puts it all into perspective. *"Do not be deceived: God cannot be mocked. A man reaps what he sows."* What are you? sowing? Are you sowing?

The stages listed below show a practical application of the truths we have already discussed. If you have ever wanted clarity or direction on how to nourish a healthy relationship, these stages will help.

There is no magic here, rather a guide to turn us to God, trust in His truth, ask for His wisdom and see His will unfold before you. Once the desire is determined, these directions will add the clarity needed to make progress in the relationship maze.

THE INTRODUCTION STAGE

The movie, <u>While You Were Sleeping</u>, is a great example of the introduction stage. If you have not seen the movie, allow me to paint the picture. Through an odd set of circumstances, a woman who admires a big city businessman saves his life and is mistaken for his fiancee. While he lies in a coma, his family takes the woman in and loves her as one of their own.

The introduction stage happens at its best when the comatose businessman's brother enters the scene. There is a definite interest between the woman and the brother, but she is his brother's supposed fiancee, so he does not pursue her romantically. Nothing physical, no projecting the relationship, no confused feelings, no expectations.

The woman and the brother cross paths on several occasions and find out more and more about one another. The interest grows, but they cannot pursue these feelings due to the circumstances. It was so refreshing to see a love story that actually has some merit. Real love had a chance to grow and not be choked out by all the stuff we so often heap onto a relationship in the early stages. The businessman comes out of the coma and the truth is revealed. What was not a mistake is how the woman and the brother of the businessman got to know one another. No pressure, no anxiety, no expectations.

The introduction stage starts even before we meet someone who sparks our interest. The first part of this stage is making sure all our personal systems are in order. This point should be marked by the character qualities of the passages we have already looked at. We must embody patience (I Cor. 13:4). We should be anxious for nothing, and focused on doing what is right, pure, and lovely, expecting nothing (Phil. 4:6-8). We should set our standards for moral excellence (II Peter 1:5). This stage is for the establishment of these truths. If you are not currently dating anyone or have just begun to date, this is the stage you are in.

GOAL: The goal for the introduction stage: Guard your heart and get to know people in a variety of situations.

The book of Ruth is also a great example of the introduction stage. Boaz had his eye on Ruth, and God provided some great opportunities for them to view one another in a variety of situations.

TIME: This stage should last for at least one month before an exclusive relationship is even considered. Developing character and getting to know and encourage people. Establish moral excellence. Keep away from any physical aspects of a relationship. The physical at this point adds no lasting benefit and greatly hampers the growth of a potentially positive relationship. Stay as neutral as possible and guard your heart. Remember love is patient.

TIP: The tip for the introduction stage: Do not allow dating to be the center of your social life. Be involved and active so when a date does come along, it is not the life and death situation many make it out to be.

THE INVESTIGATION STAGE

A visit to my accountant is always a good day for me. He is a friend, and my friends look out for my well-being. One such visit revealed a much needed attitude check for me. There was a gray area with regard to how we were going to file a certain schedule to my tax return. We weighed the options and decided the best course. I told him that whatever was the most above board was the way I wanted to go. Even if it cost a few more bucks in taxes, I wanted to be certain if I was ever audited, there was no question about how forthright we were trying to be. I have been audited once, and the IRS ended up sending me a check plus interest for such a decision. It is a great feeling knowing you have been as honest and open as possible with nothing to hide. That concept is the essence of the investigation stage.

This stage is not about running an FBI background check. This is a time to open up, be honest and hide nothing. Looking back, Heather and I agree this stage was a great time of growth for both of us. We had made a decision independent of one another that later surfaced as a key to our moving forward.

She stated it best one night when she explained, "I was so tired of being what I thought someone else was looking for in a spouse. After another painful relationship, I decided the next person I date will see the real me. Take it or leave it; I am going to be myself." God had been working in my life as well and I had established the same creed. What freedom! Yet the potential for the uncomfortable certainly exists.

There is a tendency in the investigation stage to put forth everything good and hide anything bad. This stage is an opportunity to be real with one another. The scriptures we looked at earlier approach love through openness and honesty. The directions to love in II Peter 1:5-7 go right through knowledge. Philippians 4:8 describes the first two key character qualities of love as truth and honesty. I Corinthians 13:6 is so clear in defining love as someone who rejoices in the truth. Many people, single and married, try to live a lie, and put up a front that is destined to fail, and then what?

God desires that we be free. Free from our past and free from impossible expectations. Many people are trying very hard to be something they are not. Howard Hendrick put it beautifully when he said, "We spend money we don't have to buy things we don't need to impress people we don't like." We will not enjoy any relationship the way God intended until we make a commitment to being completely open and honest with those we care about.

What a joy to reach a point in any relationship with the confidence to say, "This is who I am. I know I am not perfect, and God is still working on me, but I am free to be who He made me to be." The investigation stage is 90% inward and only about 10% outward. Yes, we need to be honest with ourselves and with those with whom we wish to invest our time. To put it simply, the biggest question to ask in this stage is, "Are we being completely open and honest with one another?"

The letter on the following page was written by a good friend and is a great example of how some people attempt to be open and honest. It is a bit extreme, but I think you will get the idea. He claims to have sent this to women after their first date.

Dear _____,

I want to thank you for the wonderful time we spent together. It truly was a great (day/evening/weekend). I enjoyed (lunch/dinner/ the movie/miniature golf/ice skating) only because I spent it with you.

_____, allow me to be completely transparent with you. You are very special to me. You are so different than all of the other (girls / women) that I've gone out with. You have the most beautiful (blue / brown / green / hazel / other_____) eyes, not to mention your gorgeous (blonde / brown / black / red / other_____) hair.

However, I don't want you to think that I only like you because of your physical appearance. What I like most about you is that you are such a strong (Christian / Buddhist / Hindu / atheist / student / cheerleader / other_____).

I hope this letter hasn't been too personal for you. I'm such a sensitive guy that sometimes I go overboard when I meet a (girl / woman) like you. I hope that we can get together again (soon/in the near future/after I've had some time to mature). Until then, I will be (praying / meditating / offering sacrifices / thinking happy thoughts) for you.

(Love / Sincerely / Yours truly / Regrettably),
Jimmy Wolfe

I hope you have never received a letter like this. The investigation stage is all about being genuine. Here are some guidelines for this stage.

GOALS: Goals of the Investigation stage: Create an open and honest environment without expectations. Allow him or her to see the real you.

TIME: This stage should last a minimum of three to four months. Allow time to reveal and grow character. There is no rush. It is certainly normal for this stage to take much more than four months.

TIP: During this stage there may be a tendency to want to skip through it. Don't! Take your time. Three months is not a long time compared to the rest of your life. Honesty and openness take time to happen.

BIG TIP: If someone is trying to project the relationship during this stage let that be a big red flag. After a couple months it is too early to say for certain if a relationship is ready to move on. If you think it is ready now, then you will only know better a few months later. So many couples put too much pressure on a relationship too soon. If the person projecting the relationship needs to know in the first few months where it is going, it is a bad sign. Chances are he or she is not looking for the right one, just someone. This is a good sign of someone who wants to get married, but is nowhere close to being ready for marriage.

Marriage takes endless amounts of open, honest communication. The sooner we can establish it the better. When you feel like you have shared it all, you are nearing the next stage. Many couples share with me how easily they communicate right off the bat. The beginning of a relationship is often this way because there is very little conflict. When there is no conflict, communication frequently is easy.

You will notice the transition to the next stage when you have had a really strong disagreement or two and still like each other. Another indicator is when you have opened up the worst part of your past and worked through it with the other person. When you can honestly say that you have shared it all and have nothing to hide, you are then ready for the next stage.

Let me just interject how wonderful it is to be yourself and know that someone else knows everything about you and still decides to stick around. It is a glimpse of what God has already done for us on a much larger scale.

THE DELIBERATION STAGE

The TV was on as I turned from the sink in my hotel room. The afternoon talk shows were on and I was on my way to grab the remote to switch to ESPN. Before I could get my finger on the button, the couple on stage had been introduced and the freak aspect of their lives exposed in white letters on the bottom of the screen. It seems these two had been married for 16 years, and on the show today he would find out for the first time his wife was actually...a MAN! I am not making this up.

Talk about your breakdown of open and honest communication, not to mention the lack of honest evaluation necessary to not notice a detail such as this in 192 months of marriage. Love is blind at times, but it does not have to be stupid. Almost without exception, most marriage-ending problems can be traced back to issues that could have and should have been dealt with long before the vows were taken.

When people rush through evaluation and deliberation, ignoring warning signs with the attitude, "Oh, he (or she) will change because we are in love," they are in for some major adjustments. Do you want a loving, open relationship or one that results in bitterness, hurt and regretting you ever met? This stage is to verify the truths of the investigation stage. Love is patient because time will tell. Tell what? Tell the truth.

Once in this stage you will have one of two experiences. Things will become clearer and clearer, or there will be an uneasiness for one reason or another. Time confirms or confuses. If after a few more months everything is going great and just continuing to get better, there is a good chance this is for keeps. There is no rush and there should not be pressure from either side to move forward until both sides are fundamentally ready to do so.

If you get to this stage and experience complete openness, it is likely to become a great relationship. Friends and family will probably agree. Those who know you best as a couple have the freedom to be honest, and yet their insight will also be positive. Such was the case during my deliberation stage with my wife Heather. We talked about our relationship and agreed it was going wonderfully and only getting better with time. We had had a few disagreements, but they were nothing we couldn't come to terms with, and we only felt closer afterwards.

During this talk we agreed about where the relationship was and were excited about where it was going, but did not want to rush into anything or put unnecessary pressure on ourselves. We decided to maintain course and speed and reevaluate in a few months. As we progressed through this stage, I knew things were changing as I sat at the dinner table with my parents and brother.

My last tour had been a long one, and it had been about a month since I had visited. It had been several months since I had been with my parents without Heather by my side. I knew the change was serious as the conversation quickly moved to the topic of Heather moments after I arrived.

"Where is Heather?" my mother questioned. I explained how she was away for the weekend seeing her parents, and that I had mentioned this fact on the phone only about four times, and most recently a few hours prior to my visit. "Oh, yeah," my mother sighed, "It's just so nice having her around. She is so sweet and fun to be around."

This was met with agreement from the rest of the table. "She sure is funny, and such a cute girl," my father added. In unison they added that it sure seemed strange not having her here. A bit encouraged and selfish at the same time, I looked at these people I had lived with for over twenty years and visited regularly since moving out. Remember me? I am the son. I use to be funny and fun to have around. What about me?

My parents, realizing their omission of appreciation for their eldest son ,simply said, "Well we just like having her around. She is so perfect. You would be crazy if you let her get away!" It was just the love and acceptance I was looking for.

You may have the opposite experience. Maybe there is discourse among one set of parents or the other. There may be an issue of uncertainty. Some aspect of the past pops up that hasn't been dealt with yet, or maybe you just are not sure. This happens at this stage just as often, if not more often than what happened to me. Pray though this stage. It is the best time to draw near the Lord and allow Him to direct your path. Whether there are concerns does not determine the quality of the relationship. God often uses these times to defuse future problems. The timing just may not be the best.

This is the time to fulfill the true definition of love. *"Bears all things, believes all thing, hopes all things, endures all things."* [1] If there are issues to be dealt with, be thankful for the opportunity to do it now. No issue big or small will just go away. This is the time to voice concerns and deal with anything no matter how insignificant it may seem. If there is tension within the family, show patience and ask for clarity of the real problem. Often these problems stem from minor issues blown out of proportion. Focused time and genuine effort given to any situation can almost always provide workable solutions.

The deliberation stage is a great place to establish the habit of dealing with concerns head on and keeping things out in the open. This is the stage to stand on God's promises. When we commit to doing it God's way, He makes us a huge promise, "God causes all things to work together for good to those who love God, to those called according to His purpose."[2] (Romans 8:28) We cannot go wrong when we take our time, allow time to confirm the truth, and work though any concerns that arise.

GOAL: Allow time to reveal truth. Ask for wisdom and counsel from family and friends.

TIME: Even in the best relationships between perfect people this stage should last a minimum of 4 months. Again, longer is better.

TIP: Remember time confirms or confuses. Ask the question, "Is this growing toward and will it result in a Galatians 5 relationship?"

ANOTHER TIP: Some relationships never make it to this stage. I do not mean they end before this stage can happen. I mean several couples date for a long time and never deal with concerns or problems. They just hope they will go away. If you are in a relationship that has gone on for several months, both sides desire to move forward, but you seem to be in a rut, there is a good chance you have never even entered the investigation stage. Start opening up. Go back a couple pages and read through that stage together. Talk about any of the aspects of love with which you struggle. If you need a topic to spur on conversation, read this book together and share how you feel about the different ideas. Whether you agree or disagree, it will be a good exercise in openness and honesty.

THE ENGAGEMENT STAGE

If you are not currently seeing someone on a regular basis, this stage would be a good one to skip over for now and refer back to later. You may want to glance over it for future reference, but the main point of this stage is for those who have successfully traveled through the other stages and are ready to move into the last stage before marriage. So take a peek and remember to come back when you have completed the others. If you choose to skip, go to the heading STAGES on page 102 and finish reading the chapter.

Heather and I had both experienced the best months of our lives in terms of our relationship. We had worked through some problems, shared our darkest secrets, and had honestly and patiently worked through everything we could think of before moving forward. So we decided to have another talk.

When faced with a major decision I always attempt to get away from the normal everyday stuff and confirm the facts. This decision was a no-brainier, but I wanted to double check the process and confirm one more time what the Lord was leading me through for the past several months. Expecting a quick confirmation from God, I was surprised to uncover the details God began to lay upon my heart.

One such detail was the choice I was about to make and the confidence I needed before moving on. I was impressed with the notion of not asking Heather to marry me until I was 100% ready. I should not pop the question nor should she say yes until it is a done deal. This may sound very obvious, but so much pain could be avoided if couples would not push for this point until all questions have been dealt with.

When they have been dealt with, wait a while. Then wait until both people involved can say, "What are we waiting for? We have discussed everything ten times." It is when both people can honestly say, "I know this is what I want to choose, and I am willing to wait forever if I must because you are worth it," then and only then should you proceed. Before we go off into fantasy land, remember this is for couples who have been together for awhile (a minimum of 8 or 9 months) and both are headed in this direction after individually and mutually agreeing.

There are some people out there who see someone interesting and after a couple dates find themselves at this point. Love at first sight is a great movie gimmick, but a poor way to look at a life long commitment. I will be the first to say I was flipped over my wife the first time I saw her. But real love happened when that interest just grew deeper in time, and a love at first sight became a deeper love at the 1,378th sighting.

Another detail God put on my heart was sensitivity. I know it was from the Lord because I just do not think of thoughtful details on my own. After confirming a big yes to being 100% ready in my own heart, and having talked with her in great detail over the idea of getting married, we were ready. While considering how to ask for her hand in marriage, I was impressed to consider when it would actually happen.

I had saved up for long time and was close to having the money to buy a ring. (If you have to borrow the money to buy a ring, you may need to wait longer. Nothing motivates savings like a goal.) So when do I ask her? I pondered a truly unique question, "When would it be good for her?" What a noble idea! When would she want to get engaged most? I checked the calendar, and I chose a time when she could see her parents, show off her ring, and plan the wedding.

I also remembered the countless married friends who spoke with great pain about having to register for everything and the tension it caused. With those planning factors in mind, I picked the date, planned to get plenty of sleep the night before, and it all fell into place. After the proposal and acceptance there were calls to be made.

She was so happy and excited, which was wonderful. Then my bride-to-be asked the question I was waiting for, "Oh my gosh, we have to register. When do you think you can go?" I replied that I was just so excited; how about tomorrow?

My premeditated, God-inspired response was met with great joy and much celebration from Heather. Not only did we endure the process, I actually had fun watching her get excited. I did not have a pressing desire to register for fancy plates that we would use once every three years, but it was important to her. We saw couples fussing and fighting over all sorts of things while we breezed through the whole process. I share this not as a brag on my ability to read the opposite sex. The Lord knows how inadequate I am. I share this to encourage any couple to take their time and have fun. If it means waiting to enjoy the process, wait.

When I meet engaged couples the most common phrase is, "We have to do

_____, and _____, and _____, then there is _____..." The list goes on and on. My encouragement for those who reach this stage is, no you don't have to do any of that stuff. All you have to do is both show up with a guy who can sign the marriage certificate. That is all that HAS to happen. This is an important day and all the details need to be perfect, but don't let a wedding ruin the start of your marriage.

STAGES

Hindsight is 20/20. It is so much easier to look at keeping on track with these stages after having gone through them. It is also encouraging to know they do work, and God is in the middle of them when we look for Him. This chapter will be very valuable to refer back to as you proceed through these different stages.

No matter where you are, in a relationship or not, now is the time to start focusing on the fact that God has a very specific way of doing things. In preparation for the most important stage of all, take a look at 1 Corinthians 13. While you read through this passage, ask God to show you which of these qualities need work in your life.

Verse eight begins by telling us, "Love never fails." I don't know about you, but I know I have failed on more than one occasion. That tells me that I need some work. What stage are you currently in? What areas does God want you to work on in this stage? Take some time to really meditate on each of these factors and put a check by the areas you feel God wants to, or is, working on in your life today.

I would say I am currently in the _____ stage.
These are the areas I feel God is trying to teach me about:

PATIENCE
KINDNESS
NOT JEALOUS
DOES NOT BRAG
IS NOT ARROGANT
DOES NOT ACT UNBECOMINGLY
IS NOT SELFISH
IS NOT PROVOKED
DOES NOT TAKE INTO ACCOUNT A WRONG SUFFERED
DOES NOT REJOICE IN UNRIGHTEOUSNESS
REJOICES IN THE TRUTH
BEARS ALL THING
BELIEVES ALL THINGS
HOPES ALL THINGS ENDURES ALL THINGS

[1]1Corinthians 13:7

CHAPTER ELEVEN

Completely Trusting

Pursuit Principles

*I*t happens every four years to anyone in the state of Georgia who wants to operate some kind of motor vehicle. It was time to renew my license and I had the perfect plan. I'd drop off Heather's car at the repair shop (someone decided to run a red light and reconstruct the front side of her car), have a friend take me to the car rental place, and finally cruise by the new "express renewal" post and be completely done by lunch to properly enjoy my birthday.

The first step came off without a hitch. On to the car rental. That's when the fun began. After filling out countless forms and promising them my first born male child, I was ready for my next chore until... "Excuse me Mr. Kington, but did you know your license expires today?" said the surprised clerk holding the keys to my freedom.

I confirmed his observation and shared with him my plan to have my license renewed and explained how the license was good at least until midnight. "This rental is for 24 hours and your license will be void for part of your rental if for any reason you cannot renew. I cannot rent you this car."

To make a long story somewhat shorter, my friend ran me over to the express renewal location which of course had major computer problems. After forty-five minutes the express renewal post had not even processed one person in the line of over twenty. I was number eighteen. We proceeded to the main license office some twenty-five minutes away only to realize it was closed on Mondays. Of course my birthday was on a Monday.

We traveled back to the express renewal location to find the line had not moved in the past hour and was now longer, and I was late for my lunch appointment. One futile attempt after another and I gave up on getting a new license for Monday.

The next day I got up early dropped my wife off at work and set out to become a legal driver once again. Another marathon line and close encounter with the wonders of technology and speed of a bureaucracy that supposedly makes life easier. I finally had my new license!

There were several times I considered just being a renegade and going without a valid operating license. My conscience and luck combined would not allow it, so I persevered and now I have the official certificate to drive.

I actually pondered during the ordeal why it was happening.

I remember praying, "Lord why can't everything go smoothly and allow me to enjoy my birthday?" (As if being born has special privileges and rights that should accompany it.) The question that continued to come to mind was, "Is it worth it? Was all the hassle worth the privilege of driving?"

I evaluated the options and quickly decided it beat the alternatives by a long shot. Sure I would much rather drive than walk, ride my bike, run, take the bus, or any combination of the above. Yes it is actually worth the runaround, the lines, the aggravation.

Many people philosophically agree with the ideas of what God's truth says about relationships. Many will even read this book and intellectually agree with most if not all of its premise. The frustration comes when we have to live it out in our day to day lives. Proverbs 3:5-7 says, *"Trust in the Lord with all your heart and lean not on your own understanding. In all your ways acknowledge Him, and He will make your path straight."* We must come to the point where we decide yes, it is worth trusting His way over what I think, feel, or reason.

In relationships, this place of completely trusting is initially uncomfortable. Case in point–Chapter 7. A young man came up to me after I had spoken on the material in Chapter 7. With a perplexed look on his face he asked me about the first question God laid upon my heart as a guideline, "You don't mean to act like I already have a girlfriend do you?" I told him no. His face relaxed for a moment.

"I mean act like you already have a wife." His face hit the floor and reflected the same feeling I had when I first thought carefully of the idea of acting as if you are taken and one day you will be. "But, then I won't have any control." Exactly! When that feeling hit me like a brick, God began to encourage me with the fact that He must be in complete control for His perfect will to be a part of my life. I must learn to completely trust Him.

While running one day I saw a wonderful picture of what complete trust looks like. The river I run along has a few bridges that span creeks. While running up to one such bridge and then over it, I came across a father and his one-year old son. The son was standing on the handrail while the father held tightly to his shirt and trousers. The father would allow his son to lean forward and hang in the balance over the water while the son shrieked with joy and laughter.

The father pulled his son back and enjoyed the moment with him. They repeated this while I jogged by.

Though the bridge was only about seven feet high, I began to figure out how high that would be compared to you and me, roughly fifty feet. Now imagine standing on a ledge fifty feet up; a friend grabs you tightly by the belt and says, "Go ahead, lean out, I've got you!" I have some strong friends that love me very much, but I would have to say no! I don't think so. There are so many variables, I just don't trust my life to someone in that situation. It's not worth it. But to a little boy who trusted that his father was in complete control, it was the time of his life! Joy beyond measure!

Our God is infinitely trustworthy, and when He says to trust in Him with ALL your heart and in ALL your way acknowledge Him, we can take Him at His word. I am afraid my way is quite different. Mine is too often to look at what I understand and what I think and what I want and ask God to give me All His resources to do what I determine needs to be done. I hope you see as you read this how ludicrous that sounds.

One of the first determinations we have to make is that we don't know everything, but He does. I must come to Him for the answers and trust that His way is, will be, and always has been better than anything I could come up with.

This concept was never more obvious then when a friend and I decided to start a workout program. We met at the gym and he asked, "What do you think we should do?" I am a man so I have an answer to any question (I did not say I have the right answer just an answer). I answered with my thoughts and insights on a balanced workout and in about two minutes exhausted my knowledge of the topic. The plan was set. We worked out anyway.

The drive home after our exercise was a bit humbling. As I reflected on the workout I realized some painful realities. First, he had beaten me at every competitive exercise. I don't like to lose and God chose to use this to get my attention. Then God began to prompt my thoughts to help me realize how selfish and deeply rooted my lack of complete trust.

Looking at Tom, (the friend I had worked out with) he is taller, stronger, and in far better shape. Tom played college football as a quarterback and has maintained the physique to prove it. He rides his bike regularly and basically puts me to shame as an athlete. I am in shape; it is just that my shape is more oblong and soft. I make it one trip up and down the basketball court and I am looking for oxygen. I realized while driving home as God whispered in my heart, "Kenn who needs to be deciding what workout to do, you or Tom?"

If I desire to get into better shape I might want to start listening and stop talking. If I genuinely desire to be in a growing , loving, fulfilling relationship, I need to quit telling God what to do and start trusting His truth that has been proven over the course of time. We must make the transition from trusting our own thoughts, feeling, and abilities, to completely trust the all-knowing trustworthy God of all.

To completely trust does not mean merely seeing what to trust; trust is an action. We do not completely trust anything until we act upon that trust. Too many people sit on the sidelines knowing what is right, hearing God's truth every week, and agreeing that what He says is true, but never making the transition from their minds into their lives.

The reason most church members today look like they just sucked on a bad lemon instead of appearing to have been filled with the abundant life provided them through Christ, because they do not act on the truth they already know. The problem with most relationships is not that we don't know enough, but it is not doing enough of what we already know to be right. We cannot say we completely trust God's truth until we start acting upon it.

God's truth is not unlike the greatest amusement park ride. We cannot and will not enjoy a roller coaster until we get on it. We can sit outside, watch, and say, "Wow, that looks like fun." We may even get closer and stand at the end of the ride watching people come off and hearing them recount the different turns and hills. Listening closely, we hear the distant screams and laughter as the train roars up, down, and around the tracks.

As observers we can even agree with one another and proclaim, "Roller coasters are fun!!" However, we simply can't enjoy the thrill of a roller coaster unless we get in line and actually get on the ride. Only then will we experience the anticipation of the first hill, the rush of emotion wondering if this thing really is on the tracks, the fright of being completely out of control, and yet loving every minute of it. There is no real joy until you and I get on the ride.

The ride to finding real love in a relationship is no different. We may study about relationships until our eyes cross, but until we are willing to completely trust that truth and start putting it into practice, it is worthless. Completely trusting means just that, completely. Too often I have started the process and after a few failures or difficult circumstances, it's back to learning more and just forgetting about the application. We just hope some of the truth rubs off on us and by osmosis becomes part of us and renders the results we desire. It's just not going to happen! Is it easy? No. Will we falter? Yes. Is it natural? No. Is it worth it? YES!

How do we get on the relationship roller coaster of Completely Trusting? By taking what we have already gone over in the previous chapters and keep putting it into our lives. Daily we must take a portion and ask God how we can live it today. Look at I Corinthians 13: 4-7 and ask God to show you which of the fifteen qualities of love to embody today. Look at Philippians 4:8 and ask God which qualities you need to be dwelling on today. Look at II Peter 1:5-8 and ask God to show you which actions need to increase in your life today. We must come to the point where practicing God's truth becomes second nature. It is when we practice His truth that we will establish our complete trust in Him and begin to experience the fulfillment, joy, peace, and other attributes God always intended us to experience.

My wife and I recently experienced roller coasters for the first time in several years. As we entered the park, I was excited and could only remember the thrills. As a ten year old, my friend and I would go to the park early and ride until the fireworks were over and the park closed. That thrill was replaced with reality on the first hill of the first ride. I began to question the construction of the structure. The safety of the ride was heavy on my mind. The height we had climbed to was way more than I remembered. Instead of raising both hands in a symbol of freedom, I gripped the lap bar with white knuckles. Why? Why was I siting in total discomfort while two teenagers in front of me laughed with their hands in the air with reckless abandon as I once did? They were accustomed to the ride. God is wooing us to trust Him with that same abandon and experience the same joy. Wait in the line (know His truth). Get on the ride (Put His truth into action). Ride it for all it is worth (See that He is completely trust worthy).

CHAPTER TWELVE

Diligently Waiting

*A Need For Personal Evaluation
And Practical Application*

*H*ave you ever received bad service at a restaurant? I mean really bad. One restaurant topped them all for me. It got to the point of actually being funny. The setting is simple enough. Heather and I were grabbing a bite between speaking engagements. We were not in a rush but neither was our waitress.

After wondering if we had mistakenly sat in the Bermuda Triangle, our waitress decided to break away from her friends and stop by our table. We had decided to go ahead and order more than just our drinks for the fear that we might not see our little helper again. It was a good decision too. She decided to vanish again after dropping off our drinks, and we began to wonder if we had been forgotten.

About thirty minutes later she surfaced again and asked if we needed anything. Dinner, would be nice. "Oh", she said, "I'll be right back with that." Our glasses also had been long since drained of any liquid when what was supposed to be our dinner arrived. Our favorite item from this particular restaurant was their fries. We'd ordered double fries and had gotten none. She dropped the plates on the table and headed away asking rhetorically, "Is there anything else you need?"

"My fries would be nice, and if we could get a refill on drinks that would be great." With a wink and a turn she was gone again. A several minutes later she looked at our table while passing by.

"You guys need anything?"

" Yeah, some refills would be nice and my fries?"

"Oh, sure," with a smile she said, "I'll have that right out for you."

Once again she asked as she passed by, "Anything else?"

"Could I get you to check on my fries?"

"Sure thing!" She smiled, winked and walked away.

Don't get me wrong, I was happy to have the ice to chew on and the burger, but after waiting well over an hour it didn't seem too much to ask for what I had ordered.

To top it off, I watched her walk away from our table and go straight to where her friends were standing. There they stood not even close to the kitchen and my long forgotten fries. She never even checked.

After investing a small portion of our lives, we had to go. I motioned for her and she made time in her busy schedule to stop by our table. "Was everything alright? Can I get you two anything else?" she said with a sincere smile and a wink.

"No, we sort of need to get going, so if we could get the check that would be all. Oh, we never got our fries so if you could knock those off the bill that would be good."

"Oh, do you want them to go?" she actually said with concern.

"No, I really don't have the time now. She was back in about five more minutes and we were off. The fries that never showed up. The sincere waitress who never put one and one together.

Heather and I laughed about that for days. Her continual, "Can I get you anything?" and smile, wink, walk away was unbelievable.

It was a few days after that when I ran across James 1:22. I wanted to have it mounted and give it to our waitress friend. But prove yourselves doers of the word and not merely hearers who delude themselves. It was at that time the phrase "wait upon the Lord" took on an entirely new meaning. I realized with great pain that this waitress had illustrated how I often approached the Lord; how I "wait on Him."

With a pure heart I say, Lord teach me your truth. Show me Your way. What in my life needs to change? Then in the most sincere way possible, I agree in my heart with His truth, smile, wink, and turn to go on my way completely forgetting what just happened. For too long I suffered from a condition that so many struggle with. We want to serve God. We desire to experience relationships and all parts of life the way He intended, but we fail to put one and one together. The results in transforming our relationships (or lack of) will not come from increasing the amount of knowledge we have about them. Results will come when we begin to diligently wait upon the Lord.

We must learn to shift our view of waiting from an outward observation of which we have no control to an inward evaluation for change. If you can picture in your mind coming to the Lord each day as a waiter or waitress, "Lord, what would you like me to change in my life today? What area of my character needs work? Father, what verse do I need to embody more today?" Then take His truth as an effectual doer and not a forgetful hearer. In every passage we have gone over in this book the principle of diligently waiting is the foundation.

In II Peter 1:5 the key to the process of love is given, *"Now for this very reason also, applying all diligence..."*[1] I Corinthians 13:7 describes one of the most important aspects of love as, *"endures all things."* In Philippians 4:9, Paul exhorts with the character of love by proclaiming, *"The things you have learned and received and heard and seen...practice these things."*[2] We see clearly that diligently waiting is far from a passive, uncontrollable wish.

This whole book has been committed to this exercise. Relationships the way God intended them have very little to do with the external forces on our lives: Who will it be? Where will we meet? How will it happen? When will it happen? Godly relationships have everything to do with the internal restructuring God desires us to embrace. Take his truth and do it. Don't stop at hearing it, agreeing with it, talking about it, or theoretically proving it. Let those aspects be the catalyst to obediently, practically, with endurance, diligently doing it.

I am so encouraged and excited for those of you who have made it here. We must realize this is not the end but simply part of the process. Those who will diligently wait on the Lord will discover the relationship He has in store.

What lies ahead?

Well, there is hard news and great news. If you have not yet discovered, the process is not easy and the complete results are not instantaneous. Philippians 1:6 is my admonition to you as you strive for God's best with all your heart, *"He who began a good work in you will perfect it until the day of Christ Jesus."*[3]

There will be times where nothing seems to be going right as you apply these truths. Take heart. That simply means it is working. Waiting diligently means we will not always bring the right order to the table every time. God is the most patient, understanding customer. Reproof is part of the process. Proverbs 12:1 puts it best, *"Whoever loves discipline, loves knowledge, but he who hates reproof is stupid."*[4] That is the hard news.

Now for the great news. The results are promised by the only one who can keep such promises. When we commit our lives to diligently waiting upon Him, He makes us some pretty awesome guarantees. Those who wait upon the Lord will gain new strength (Is. 40:31). Those who abide in the perfect truth of God will be blessed...(James 1:25).Through prayer and practice we are promised we will have the protection and peace of God (Phil. 4:6-7).

As the faithful Lord of all continues to refine your heart and life, revisit these truths regularly. Review what you have written and see the growth that is taking place.

Thank you for allowing me to be a part of your process. My prayer is for God to continue to mold you into becoming worthy of the love you are looking for!

[1]NAS
[2]NAS
[3]NAS
[4]NAS

DAILY
Devotional

DAILY DEVOTION

☐

Week 1

What Is Love
Read Chapters 1-4 this week.

Day One:

Read John 15:13, Luke 22:42-44, Romans 5:8

- According to these verses how committed is God's love toward you?

- How does it make you feel to know God cares that much about you?

Read: John 3:17

- Why did God send His son Jesus?

Tonight:

Write down the best thing you did today? Now, write down the worst thought or action you did today (Use code if you don't want to write it out). Read Romans 5:8 again.

Day Two:

Read Jeremiah 29:12, 33:3

- Getting Real with God is like any other relationship. What does God desire from us?

Read Matthew 22:37

- What kind of commitment does God require for us to fully enjoy His love?

Tonight:

If the time you spent with God today was the same as the time you spent with someone you were interested in how would he or she feel about you today? What is one way you could improve?

Day Three:

Read Matthew 22:39, John 13:34-35

- Put these verses into your own words.

Read Galatians 5:13

- If love is expressed through service what are some ways you can serve today?

Tonight:

What are some ways you served today expecting NOTHING in return?

Day Four:

Read John 3:16

- "For God so loved the world that He _____..."

- What did God give and why?

Tonight:

What have you given in the past few days of value to another (Time, Encouragement, Help, etc.)

Day Five:

Read Proverbs 17:17

- When are true love and friendship proven?

- Read Acts 20:35

- Put this verse into your own words.

Tonight:
Who can you serve by helping tomarrow?

Day Six:

- Review all the truths from this week. Do you remember the definition of Love?

- Love is a _____ _____to _____
  _____ and _____ _____.

- ?How did you attempt to live this definition this week?

DAILY DEVOTION

☐

Week 2

Fundamental vs. Supplemental Intimacy
Read Chapter 5 this week.

Day 1

Read John 10:10, John 14:6

- What is the only way our fundamental intimacy need can be met?

- What is the only way we will experience abundant life?

- What is one step you can take today to improve your weakest area of love?

Tonight:
What did you do to improve?

Day 2

Memorize Proverbs 3:5-6

- According to these verses is it more important to trust God or understand circumstances?

- What does it mean to trust God vs. trusting what we understand?

Tonight:
What did you do today to improve your weakest area of the love definition?

Day 3

Read Matthew 28:20, Hebrews 13:5

- What two absolutes does God promise us that we are incapable of promising one another?

Tonight:

Recall a time today you felt God's presence most and least. Re-read today's verses.

Day 4

Read Genesis 2:18, James 1:2-5

- Why was Eve created?

- Based on James 1:2-5 does the process to becoming perfect and complete ever mention a relationship with anyone other than God? Why do you think that is?

Tonight:

Write down what trials you faced today and how you responded: Do your trials relate at all to your weakness in the love definition? How did you improve today?

Day 5

Read Philippians 4:4-7

- Which part of these verses is the biggest challenge to you with regard to relationships?

- Rejoice always,

- Gentle spirit be known,

- Anxious for nothing,

- Everything by prayer and supplication...

Tonight:

Find a way to improve that area today. Write down what happened:

Day 6

- Review this weeks devotions. How did you or could you apply the truth you learned this week?

- What steps did you take to improve on your weakness in the love definition?

- Have you memorized Proverbs 3:5-6 perfectly?

- Review this weeks CORE Group questions (You do NOT have to answer them just read them.)

Week 3

Road Map to LOVE?
Read Chapter 6 this week

Day 1

Read Philippians 4:8-9.

- Rank these qualities from your strongest to your weakest.

- Take one of the lowest and ask God to help you improve on it today.

Tonight:

What happened in that area today? What did you learn or how did you improve?

Day 2

Memorize Philippians 4:8 today.

- Put it on a card and read it every time you eat.

- Read it every time you change your clothes.

- Quote this verse to at least two people before you go to bed tonight.

Tonight:

Did you quote the verse to two people? What quality sticks out in your mind? Why?

Day 3

Read II Peter 1:5-9

- Review the qualities that lead to LOVE. Rank your self from 1 to 10 (10 being the best).

- Moral Excellence ___, Knowledge ___, Self-Control ___,

- Perseverance ___, Godliness___, Brotherly Kindness ___.

- Where are you relationally according to these standards?

- Ask God to help you move forward today?

Tonight:

What area do you think God wanted to work on today?
What happened?

Day 4

Memorize Philippians 4:9 today.

- Write it on the back of the card verse 8 is on.

- Review Phil 4:8-9 and II Peter 1:5-9. Ask God to show you which area needs the most work.

- Limit to 1 or 2. Practice the quality today.

Tonight:

How did you improve or what did you learn?

Day 5

Read Galatians 5:13

- Touch base with someone in your group today. Practice saying your memory verses to him or her.

- Share what you have learned in one or more areas.

- Ask what areas God has been working in his or her life.

- Commit to pray for them today and to grow in your weakness before your next meeting.

Tonight:

Write down how it made you feel to encourage someone else. How did it feel to know someone else is trying too?

Day 6

Take a blank sheet of paper.

- Close your book and bible.

- Write from memory Proverbs 3:5-6 & Philippians 4:8-9

- Check how you did. Were the verses word perfect?

- Review the CORE group questions for your next meeting.

DAILY DEVOTION

☐

Week 4

Time To Join AAA
Read Chapter 7 this week

Day 1

Read Galatians 5:22-23

- Out of the nine fruit which 3 are most and least evident ion your life?

    MOST:

    LEAST:

- Pick one weakness and specifically work on it today.

- Pick one of your strengths and use it to help someone who may have it as a weakness.

Tonight:

How did you work on your weakness? Who did you help with your strength and how?

Day 2

Memorize Galatians 5:22-23

- Write it down on a card and read it every time you look in a mirror.

- Share with someone in your group your weakest of the nine fruit. Pray for his or hers today.

Tonight:

Whom did you pray for?
Say the verse out loud without looking at the card.

Day 3

Review the past couple weeks

- Which truth or verses stick out in your mind?

- Write down any progress in any area you have noticed.

- Today pick an area or truth you planed on working on but fell short (busy, forgot, fell short, etc.).

Tonight:

What did you work on? How did you progress or what did you learn?

Day 4

Read Proverbs 19:22a

- Who is the last person in your day today that deserves kindness?

- Do something today to specifically show him or her kindness.

- Who in your life is someone that deserves kindness that you have neglected?

- Drop a note; give a call, or just drop by to let him or her know you care.

- Also today, do at least one random act of kindness for someone your do not know. Be creative.

- Quote Philippians 4:8-9 & Galatians 5:22-23 at least twice to prove you have memorized them.

Tonight:

Whom did you quote the verses to?
Who were you kind to and how?

Day 5

Read Philippians 2:3

- Are there any relationships in your life that are not right?

- How can you consider the person or persons more important then yourself?

- Review Gal. 5:22-23 and write down any progress you have made in any area this week.

Tonight:

What did you do today to show preference to those your mentioned earlier today?

Day 6

- Catch Up

- Go back and redo any day you missed or did not give 100%.

- If you are completely up to date pick your favorite day and repeat it.

Tonight:

Review the CORE group questions for this week and make sure you know you memory verses.

DAILY DEVOTION

☐

Week 5

Becoming A Great Lover
Read Chapter 8 this week

Day 1

- What are the top five attributes you look for in a person of the opposite sex? List them here:

- 1.   2,   3.   4.   5.

- Are you a perfect example of your own list?

Read Matthew 7:1-3

- Pick your weakest feature of yourself compared to your list and work on that today.

Tonight:

What is a way you can improve in these areas over time? In what area do you need accountability?

Day 2

Read I Corinthians 13:4-7

- How many qualities of love are listed here?

- Rank yourself from 1 to 10 in each area.

- What area is your worst and which is your best?

- Practice both today.

Tonight:

How did you specifically grow in the two areas from this morning?

Day 3

Memorize I Corinthians 13:4-7

- Take the next worst and next best qualities from yesterday and grow in those areas today.

- What specifically can you do to improve?

- Pray and ask God for wisdom and direction on how to improve.

Tonight:

What areas were you to focus on today? What did you do to improve? How did it go?

Day 4

Review all the memory verses and continue to memorize I Corinthians 13:4-7

- Pick two more qualities to work on today.

- How do you intend to improve them?

Tonight:

How did you do?

Day 5

- Try to write down all the qualities mentioned in I Cor. 13:4-7 without looking:

- Whichever one(s) you forgot, focus on that one or ones today.

- If you remembered them all pick two you have not worked on this week and improve today.

- Quote the memory verses to two people today.

Tonight:

What areas did you work on? How did it go? Did you quote your verses? If NO, Call someone in your group and quote it to them.

Day 6

Read I Corinthians 13

- What areas have you not worked on yet?

- Make a specific effort to grow in those areas today.

- Ask God to show you the areas that need the most improvement.

- Ask someone to hold you accountable weekly to work on your weaknesses.

Tonight:

Decide what you need the most work on. Who would be a good person to share this with to hold you accountable? Get in touch with him or her within the next 24 hours.

DAILY DEVOTION

Week 6

An Attitude of Gratitude
Read Chapter 9 this week

Day 1

Read Luke 6:35

- Put these verses into a mordern, personal form.

- Where do you think the reward for such attitudes comes from?

- Who is a person you will encounter today that you do not really like?

- What can you do good or give to him or her today expecting nothing in return?

- Write down a couple ideas, pick one and do it (Keep it very simple).

Tonight:

What did you do and for whom? Describe how he or she reacted. How did it make you feel? Be Honest.

Day 2

Memorize Philippians 2:3

- What are some ways you think or act selfish?

- Ask God to show you one selfish attitude or action that you could work on.

- Today look for opportunities to grow.

Tonight

What were some situations where you showed preferance to others? What were some situations where you failed?

Day 3

Take a blank sheet of paper

- Write down all the verses you have memorized. See how many you can get word perfect.

- Pick the verse that has taught you the most.

- Pick the quality or attitude that you have noticed the most progress in from that verse.

- Ask God to teach you even more and focus on that quality again today.

- Share with someone the verse and the quality you see changing in your life.

Tonight:

How did you grow in that area today? Who did you share the verse and quality with?

Day 4

Review Phil. 4:5-9. Gal. 5:22-23, I Cor. 13:4-7, II Peter 1:5-9

- From all these passages which area of your life has been the toughest to change?

- Pick a quality from one of these verses and focus on that area today.

Tonight

How did it go?

Day 5

Review all the verses memorized.

- Quote them all to someone in your group today.

- Share with someone which truth has meant the most to your growth and why?

- Pick one quality from your favorite verse and ask God to make it real to you today.

Tonight

Who did you quote the verses to? Which quality did you pick and what happened today to make it real?

Day 6

- By this point many of these questions may seem redundant. The truth is that real growth does not take place by reading a verse and agreeing with it's premiss. Real growth happens when we put the truth into our lives and allow it to take root in our hearts. We will be ready for the relationship of a lifetime only when we break through the surface of God's truth and allow it to change the very core of who we are.

- Today go back to any day's devotion (weeks 1-6) and do it again.

- Ask God to open your eyes to a new depth.

Tonight:

What was different this time? Was it a deeper view of the same truth or a new area to work on altogether?

DAILY DEVOTION

☐

Week 7

A Plan & A Promise
Read Chapter 10 "NOW"

Day 1

Read Chapter 10

Tonight:

Finish reading chapter 10 if your have not already.

Day 2

Read Psalms 46:10

- What stage (from Chapter 10) are you currently in?

- Do you agree or disagree with the Goal, Time, and Tips of your stage? Explain your answer.

- What truth sticks out as most important in that particular stage?

- What stage do you or have you struggled with the most?

- Identify a truth from that stage and focus on it today.

Tonight:

What truth did you apply today and how? What stage do you think the members of your CORE group are in?

Day 3

Read II Peter 1:5-8

- Do you see a correlation to the stages mentioned in ch. 10 and these verses?

- Which part of II Peter 1:5-7 is your weakest?

- How can you improve on it today?

Tonight:
List the action(s) you took to improve.

Day 4

- Write a synopsis of your growth over the past few weeks.

- Have you mastered the character and qualities mentioned in all the verses?

Read Proverbs 24:16

- Determine for the rest of the week to make progress and not give up.

- Ask God to help you move to the next level of understanding.

Tonight:
What area do you desire to improve most? Go to sleep thinking of the purest example of what you would be like with that improvement.

Day 5

Memorize Proverbs 24:16

- Describe what you would be like if your greatest area of struggle was your greatest strength.

- What is one step you can take to improve that area today (Be simple & practical)?

Read Proverbs 27:17

- Set up a time to meet with a CORE group member and share your progress.

- Share your greatest strengths and your greatest area of change.

Tonight:

What step did you take today? Who are you meeting with and when?

Day 6

Read Proverbs 17:17

- How important is it to have friends help keep you on track relationally?

- What specifically can you do to keep on track and keep growing in the truths you have been learning?

- Today be a good friend.

Tonight:

How were you a good friend?

Week 8

Completely Trusting & Diligently Waiting
Read Chapter 11 this week

Day 1

Read Proverbs 3:3-4

- Do you ever struggle with telling the whole truth or doing what you know is right?

- Today look for opportunities to stand on truth and not compromise.

- Today, also, find at least three ways to show kindness.

- At least one act of kindness to a stranger or anonomously.

Tonight:

Give an example of how you were honest or stood up for truth. List the ways you were kind.

Day 2

Read Proverbs 3:5-6

- What area(s) of your life is it most difficult to trust God 100%.

- What do you think or know God says about that area?

- How can you aknowledge God in that area (Be specific)?

- Share your action with someone and ask him or her to hold you accountable to do it.

Tonight:

Who did you confide in to keep you accountable?

Day 3

Read James 1:21-25

- What do you think the word planted (or implanted)in verse 21 means?

- Put the main idea of these verses into your own words.

- Review all the memory verses. What truth do you need to apply most today?

- Look for ways to specifically take action in that area today.

Tonight:

Where you a hearer or a doer today?

Day 4

Memorize James 1:22

- What truth or needed action comes to mind as you think of this verse?

- What is one thing you can do today to take action in that area?

Tonight:

What did you DO?

Day 5

Read Hebrews 10:23-25

- What is the central thought of these verses?

- How can you live this truth today? Think of at least one action step and do it?

Tonight:

What was your step and how did you do it?

Day 6

Read Romans 7:15-8:3

- How does this passage make you feel?

- Dwell on 8:1 today. If we do nothing right or good how does that affect our relationship to God?

Tonight:

Before you go to sleep say out loud to yourself, "God loves me." Ten times. Each time emphasis a different word. "GOD loves me; God LOVES me; God loves ME..."

Week 9

How About Those Fries?
Read Chapter 12

Day 1

Read Philippians 1:6

- What does this verse mean to you?

- How does God Perfect?

- What area do you feel God wants to work on in your life today?

Tonight:

What area did you grow in today and how?

Day 2

Read Proverbs 12:1

- According to this verse what happens is not the issue but how we handle what happens.

- How are we to face failures and correction?

- What part of your life do you feel needs the greatest correction today?

- What is one action you can take to correct that area?

Tonight:

What area-needed correction & what action did you take?

Day 3

Read Isaiah 40:28-31

- According to these verses how do you think God feels about your efforts to do relationships His way?

- According to verses 28 & 29 how does God respond to His followers?

- Look at the area you have struggled with the most over these past several weeks.

- Ask God to give you new strength and to grow that area of your life today.

Tonight:

Did you try? Rest knowing God loves your efforts regardless of the immediate result.

Day 4

Read Is. 40:31, James 1:25 & Phil. 4:6-7

- What are the results of seeking to do relationships God's way?

- What are the two or three biggest lessons you have learned over the past nine weeks?

- What verse(s) have you seen new depth to? Give an example.

- How have you specifically applied one of these lessons?

Tonight:

What opportunities did you have today to apply the truth mentioned earlier today?

Day 5

Observe today with new eyes.

- Ask God to help you see the difference(s) in your life over the past several weeks.

- Today look for the changes in attitudes and actions that you think have taken place.

Tonight:

Write down as many areas of growth in your life that have taken place. Remember, if you specifically try to grow in an area then growth is happening. Growth happens due to commitment and action not feelings.

Day 6 Review

- What Truth(s) do you think will make the biggest difference in your relationships?

- What do you think are the most helpful lessons learned from:

    The book:

    Daily devotions:

    CORE group:

Tonight:

Rest knowing you are growing. You are becoming the love you are looking for. Congratulations!

Group Chapter Reviews and Questions

CORE GROUP

Introduction Week

Getting To Know One Another

- Open on time, on your knees, in Prayer
- Review what a CORE Group is. (Read next page)
- Determine the meeting Logistics.
- Sign commitment.
- Answer the questions as a group

A CORE Group is 3 to 7 people committed to learning, applying, and growing in the truth. Deciding to be a part of this CORE group means your will be:

Committed
Open
Responsible
Encouraging

You are Committing to being prepare each week. You are committing to being on time to the meetings. You are also committing to being open, responsible, and encouraging each week with those in your group. This commitment will be for 9 more weeks, and it will take approximately 30 to 45 minutes each day to complete the reading, devotions, and memory work. If you do not plan on being at all the meetings or do not feel you will have time to do the assignments DAILY, please wait until a time when you can.

The commitment of this CORE group is not just logistical. You should commit to being open and honest. Real growth only happens when an atmosphere of openness exists. True openness will not occur unless each member of the group is committed to being responsible. Responsible with the information shared and keeps it confidential. Responsible to show grace and compassion as failures and frustrations are shared. Responsible to encourage. Not to encourage simply with words during time together in the group, but with actions on a regular basis. A commitment to stay it touch with CORE group members, pray for each others weaknesses, encourage by being accountable and holding accountable in times of need.

The relationship transformation this type group envokes is not superficial, but changes that effect the very core of who we are.

If you are willing to make such a commitment determine the day, time, and place you agree to meet. Print your name in the blanks provided and sign the commitment. *(see next page)*

MY CORE GROUP COMMITMENT

Day: _____

Time: _____

Place: _____

I _____ _____ hereby commit to the above day, time, and place to complete this material with my CORE group. I will be Committed, Open, Responsible, and Encouraging.

Witnesses: _____
               _____
               _____
               _____

Signature: _____

Introduction Week CORE Group Questions:

1. Each person in the group describe your first date, first kiss, or Jr. High crush.

2. Name someone or something you love and what that means.

3. Be responsible to being confidential. Share a personal example of a confidence betrayed or a secret revealed. What happened?

4. Write down on a piece of paper something that no one in the group would ever guess about you (Ex. You've been hang gliding or went somewhere famous; be creative). Put all the pieces of paper in a hat then read them out loud. After all have been read try to guess who did what.

5. Close in Prayer. Pray silently for the person on your right and left. Ask God to give wisdom and insight as you go through this material. Have someone close the prayer after a few moments.

NEXT WEEK:

Read Chapters 1-4
Do Week 1 Daily Devotions
Look over the CORE group questions for next week.
You do not have to answer them. Just review them.

CORE GROUP

Week 2

• Open on time, on your knees, in prayer.
• Open your books to Week 1 daily devotions to show the work is done.
• Answer Week 2 CORE group questions as a group

Week 2 CORE Group Questions:

1. What is the best thing that happened to you this week?

2. Take a few minutes each and describe your family life growing up?

3. If the media (Movies, Magazines, and TV) defined love what would the definition be?

4. Turn to page 7. How did you define love?

5. What is the 11 word LOVE definition covered in chapters 1-4?

6. Which of the three parts of that definition is the most unnatural for you personally?

7. What truth or illustration from chapters 1-4 sticks out in your mind the most? Why?

8. What day's devotion and / or nights action step sticks out in your mind? Why?

9. Pick your weakest part of the love definition. How can you improve in that area this week?

    Write down each day what you did to try to improve.

10. Close in prayer. Pray for the person on your left and right; pray specifically for any weaknesses or struggles.

NEXT WEEK:

Read chapter 5

Memorize: **Proverbs 3:5-6**
(Each week everyone memorize the same version)

Do week 2 daily devotions

Improve your weakest area of LOVE
(Write daily what you did to improve you weakness.)

Review CORE group questions for next week.
(You do NOT have to do them. Just review)

Encourage at least two people in your CORE group in their area of weakness.

CORE GROUP

Week 3

- Start on time, on your knees in prayer.
- Everyone quote Proverbs 3:5-6 individually
- Open your books to Week 2 Daily Devotions to show you have completed the questions.
- Answer the Week 3 CORE Group questions as a group.

Week 3 CORE Group Questions:

1. What is your favorite number and why?

2. Who was one of your hero's growing up and why?

3. Share a time when you had to make a big decision and were not sure what to do. How did it turn out?

4. What are the two types of intimacy needs in our lives?

5. Who are the two sources to meet those needs?

6. Which illustration or truth sticks out in your mind from Chapter 5?

7. Which days devotion sticks out in your mind and why?

8. What actions did you take to grow this week? Be specific.

9. Did you do the Daily devotions each day?
   If YES, when and how long did it take you?
   If no, why not?

10. Why is it important to keep up daily?

11. How do our daily commitments affect our character?

12. Close in prayer. Pray each day for the person on your right. Specifically for his or her Daily Devotion time.

NEXT WEEK:

Read Chapter 6
Memorize: ***Philippians 4:8-9***
Do Week 3 Daily Devotions
Daily Devotions should be done DAILY.
This material is designed to not be time consuming but must be done day by day.
Review CORE group questions for next week.

CORE GROUP

Week 4

- Start on time on your knees in prayer.
- Everyone take turns quoting Philippians 4:8-9
- Open your book to show you have completed the daily devotions.
- Answer the Week 4 CORE Group questions as a group.

Week 4 CORE Group Questions:

1. When you were 9 years old, what did you want to be when you grew up?

2. What do you dream of becoming now?

3. What character qualities do you desire in someone of the opposite sex?

4. What truth from this week's devotions sticks out in your mind and why?

5. What part of chapter 6 stands out in your mind? Why?

6. If you graded yourself on the qualities mentioned in Phil. 4:8-9 what would your score be? (1-100)

7. What quality do you see most in the person on your right.

8. Someone read II Peter 1:5-7. Each person in the group share his or her strongest and weakest attribute.

9. What steps did you take this week to improve?

10. Close in prayer.

11. Ask God to impress one person from your CORE Group on your heart this week and pray for them daily

NEXT WEEK:

Read Chapter 7
Memorize: **Galatians 5:22-23**
Do Week 4 Daily Devotions
Review next weeks CORE Group questions.

CORE GROUP

Week 5

- Start on time on your knees.
- Show that you have done week 4 daily devotions.
- Whomever quoted the verses last week, quote Gal.5:22-23 first this week.
- Also, everyone quote Proverbs 3:5-6
- Answer the Week 5 CORE Group questions as a group.

Week 5 CORE Group Questions:

1. What is your favorite soft drink & candy bar?

2. If the person on your right were a car what would he or she be? Why?

3. How do you want your marriage to be the same as your parents?

4. How do you want it to be different?

5. Describe the fruit (Gal. 5:22-23, not apple or banana) you think the person on your left most exemplifies.

6. Which fruit of the spirit is your favorite? Why?

7. What part of chapter 7 challenged you most?

> **Act taken and one day you will be.**
> **Date to develop faithfulness.**
> **Keep special things special.**

How did it challenge you?

8. Which daily devotion was the most insightful for you?

9. Share some of the actions you took to grow this week.

10. Plan a time to share a meal and do something fun together as a group (This is mandatory).

11. Close in prayer. Pray out loud for the person on your left.

Go around until everyone has been prayed for out loud.

NEXT WEEK:

Read Chapter 8
Do week 5 daily devotions.
*Memorize: **I Corinthians 13:4-7***
Review CORE group questions for next week.

CORE GROUP

Week 6

- Start on time on your knees in prayer.
- Everyone show you have completed week 5 daily devotions.
- Quote I Corinthians 13:4-7 & Phil. 4:8-9
- Answer the Week 6 CORE Group questions as a group.

Week 6 CORE Group Questions:

1. On the count of three point to the person you think had the longest dating relationship in high school.

2. Find out the truth. Who did and how long?

3. What days action this past week sticks out in your mind?

4. Go around the group and have everyone read their day one answers from the week 5 daily devotions.

5. Do the same for day two.

6. What part of chapter 8 made the biggest impression on you?

7. Read I Cor.13:4-7 out loud.

8. Pick one person and everyone share what quality from these verses he or she thinks best describes that person.

9. Repeat this process for every person in the group.

10. Everyone share which quality you think is your weakest.

11. Close in prayer. Pray for the person on your right and left. Specifically pray for their weakest qualities.

NEXT WEEK:

Read chapter 9
Do daily devotions for week 6.
Memorize: **Philippians 2:3**
Review CORE group questions for next week.

CORE GROUP

Week 7

- Start on time on your knees in prayer
- Show your week 6 daily devotions to prove you have completed them.
- Quote Philippians 2:3 & Gal 5:22-23
- Answer the Week 7 CORE Group questions as a group.

Week 7 CORE Group Questions:

1. What are the two absolutes mentioned in chapter 9?

2. Which is your weakness and which is your natural tendency?

3. How did each of you answer the first day's devotion questions?

4. Now review day two together. Focus on the actions done to grow.

5. Randomly mention something you appreciate about one or two people in your group.

6. What is a truth or illustration from chapter 9 that made the most impact on you?

7. What is one way you took action to improve your weakest absolute this week?

8. As a group think of 10 ways you can show appreciation.

9. Take one of the ideas and tell the group which one you plan to do this week.

10. Close in prayer.

NEXT WEEK:

Read chapter 10
Do daily devotions for week 7.
Memorize Proverbs 24:16
Review CORE group questions for next week.

CORE GROUP

Week 8

- Start on time on your knees in prayer
- Open books to daily devotions week 7 to show work is done.
- Quote Proverbs 24:16 & I Corinthians 13:4-7
- Answer the Week 8 CORE Group questions as a group.

Week 8 CORE Group Questions:

1. What was you favorite subject in elementary school?
      Jr. High?   High School?

2. What is something you saved up for to buy? How long did it take?

3. What are the stages of relationships mentioned in chapter 10?

4. Take one stage at a time and discuss what is important about each stage and why?

5. What devotion day meant the most to you this week?

6. Read Proverbs 24:16.

7. How important is persistence in becoming the person God wants you to be?

8. Who in this group has shown the greatest desire to make change and not give up?

9. Close in prayer.

NEXT WEEK:

Read Chapter 11
Do week 8 daily devotions
Memorize James 1:22
Review next weeks CORE group questions.

CORE GROUP

Week 9

- Start on time on your knees in prayer
- Show week 8 daily devotion to prove work has been completed.
- Quote James 1:22 & Proverbs 3:5-6
- Answer the Week 9 CORE Group questions as a group.

Week 9 CORE Group Questions:

1. If anyone in the group has ever done a ropes course or trust games have them describe the experience.

2. Pick the two devotions from this week that challenged you the most and share your answers and actions.

3. What do you see as the main theme of chapter 11?

4. Pick one illustration from the chapter and relate it to a truth or verse.

5. Share an experience during these past few weeks where you trusted God's truth over your feelings.

6. Plan another time when you can get together as a group to share a meal and have fun together.
   (Make it a time after next weeks final CORE group meeting.)

7. Close in prayer.

NEXT WEEK:

Read Chapter 12
Finish the final week's devotions
Review all your memory verses.
Review the final week's CORE group questions.

CORE GROUP

☐

Week 10

- Start on time on your knees in prayer
- Show week 9 daily devotions to prove your work is completed.
- Quote the verse that has meant the most to you during this time.
- Quote the verse that has challenged you the most.
- Answer the Week 10 CORE Group questions as a group.

Week 10 CORE Group Questions:

1. In 5 words or less describe what you have experienced in the past 10 weeks.

2. What one main principle or truth will you take from the book?

3. What one main principle or truth will you take from the daily devotions?

4. What one main principle or truth will you take from the CORE group time?

5. What one area of your life has been changing the most?

6. What verse has meant the most to you?

7. Each person pick any one of week nine's daily devotions and share your answers and actions.
    (It can be the same day or all different)

8. What is the correlation between applying God's truth and being ready for proper relationships?

9. Share your greatest area in need of strengthening.

10. Pray for each other's needs.

NEXT WEEK:

(Optional: See next page)

CORE GROUP

30 DAYS OF LOVE

Are You Living Love?

Begin 15 Days Of Love

Begin taking one quality from I Corinthians 13:4-7 each day and live it.
Rank your self daily from 1-10 (10 being best).
At the end of 15 days add up your score.

1-40	At least you are trying. Most people never get this far.
41-85	Improvement may be needed but you are on your way.
86-125	You are on the brink of greatness. Do not stop now.
126-145	You are just about irresistible! Maintain course and speed.
146-150	You are the example to follow! Keep seeking things above!

After the first 15 days type out all 15 qualities and run off three copies. Ask 3 CORE group members to evaluate you honestly. Average each quality then add their scores together. See how they compare to your self-evaluation. Average your self-evaluation and the cumulative average of the friends' scores.

Do it for another 15 days and see if you can improve one quality at a time one day at a time. Score yourself again and see how you improve.

You may also want to consider leading a new group through this material. Going through it a second time will only sharpen your? character and reveal new strengths. Being around others who are growing and improving only benefits us on our own journey
(*Proverbs 27:17*)